THE THEATER AND I

A Chat with Facebook Friends

MARK LORD

RED
PENGUIN
Books

For Ruth and Harry Lord,

my parents,

who introduced me to the theater.

CONTENTS

INTRODUCTION

Hi! My name is Mark and I'm a theaterholic.

It's been like that most of my life, and, at this stage, I don't think it's about to change. Nor would I want it to.

I love everything that theater has brought me, and, over time, I have come to appreciate more than ever all that it has to offer the world.

This is a book that was inspired by my love of the theater, and by friends of mine who have shared their thoughts about this very topic on my Facebook page.

I guess you could say it all began many moons ago—2012, actually—when I happened to post a question about the theater. I was astounded by the great interest shown by my friends. I knew some of them were aficionados, like myself. Others have what I would consider a passing interest in it. But encouraged by the response, I raised another theater-related question the following day. And then another and another. Thus began a tradition that lasted, on and off, for 15 months. Since I equate many things with the theater, that would be about equal to the run of the original Broadway production of *Follies*, which I can proudly say I saw. More on that experience in chapter fifteen.

A couple of years later, I ran another series of questions on the same theme, which only lasted about three months—coincidentally, similar to the 2001 Broadway revival of *Follies*.

Late in 2017, I decided to revive the practice once again, this time under the formal designation, "Weekly Theater Question." As of this writing, for a year and a half, I have posted a different question on my page every Friday morning, with just a couple of missed weeks, with each one numbered sequentially. Unfortunately, no correlation here with the most recent *Follies* incarnation, which closed before its time.

The questions tend to elicit responses directly from the heart—gut feelings, you might say—leading to insightful, sometimes even heated conversations. It is around these questions (mostly culled from the latest bunch) and my friends' replies—in their own words—that much of this book is centered. I also share some of my own theatrical experiences, which I hope you find amusing, enlightening, maybe even inspirational.

I hope, too, that you will forgive me if I should happen to engage in the dropping of some boldfaced names, a near inevitability when one talks about theater. I eagerly recount the story of how **Alec Baldwin** ended up taking an exam I had given to my English class (for 29 years I was a high school teacher in the New York City public school system). I explain why **Ethel Merman** felt the need to call security on me as I approached her one day. And I reminisce about what I did that apparently intrigued **Harold Prince** the time he sat behind me at an off-Broadway play. Of course, I also include my favorite show business encounter of all—the night I had dinner with **Marlo Thomas** . . . well, sort of.

Just a word about some of the other names in boldface contained herein, the ones that might not necessarily be as recognizable: They belong to the friends I told you about. To help you get to know them—at least a little—I've offered brief words of introduction the first time each is mentioned.

A personal note to those friends, some of whom I suspect will be reading this: Please forgive me if, in the interest of literary perfection, I've taken a few slight liberties to "fix up" some of your comments . . . adding a period here, or quotation marks there, or, perhaps, spelling out words fully where you used common social media abbreviations. Hey, once an English teacher, always an English teacher!

Chapter One

HOW ABOUT A BOOK?

*O*ne of my greatest pleasures has been to see people from different aspects of my life "meeting" each other over a discussion of their personal experiences and observations as ordinary theatergoers.

But how, exactly, did this book come about? To mark the first-year anniversary of the latest "revival run" of my Facebook questions, I invited my friends to turn the tables and ask ME their favorite theater questions. One of them came from **Michele Gerrig Newmark**, whom, along with her husband, **Alan Newmark**, I met through a mutual friend, **Larry Gold**, who was often in the orchestra pit and occasionally on stage for our local musical productions. By the way, "local" for me largely refers to Queens, one of the five boroughs of New York City, where I've lived for most of my life. Anyhow, over the years, the Newmarks have rarely missed a show on Broadway or off, or any of the productions I've been involved in. From Michele came this query: "Have you thought of compiling some of the questions/answers into a book?"

It had an old familiar ring to it. "Was it you who asked me this before," I wrote back, "or are there two people out there who think it would be a good idea?"

Another friend, **Michael Brooks**, who for years has been involved as a show producer and performer with the Patio Players of the Plainview Jewish Center on Long Island, a group I've worked with quite frequently, wrote back: "I asked you Mark, a while ago."

And so he had! I got to know Michael through yet another friend, **Robert Cohen**, who asked me to help resuscitate the group after many years of inactivity. Back in September of 2018, Michael had written me a private message, advising, "Make sure to keep a record of all your theatre questions. A book is in the future."

Who knew he was so prophetic?

In response to Michele's question, I thought I was being funny when I said, "I'd love to do it. Now, to find a publisher. LOL." (Yes, even English teachers use that particular abbreviation!)

Shortly thereafter I received the following private message from a woman named **Stephanie Sands Larkin**: "Funny you were just commenting online about looking for a publisher—I am a publisher and **JK** [her son] and I were just talking last week about how we thought that your theater questions and insights would make a fun book. We planned to make a date to sit down with you about the possibilities, if you are game."

As it happened, the Larkins, long-time friends of mine whose entire family had seemingly been involved in community theater, had started their own publishing company, Red Penguin Books. A glimpse at the back cover of this publication will offer evidence as to where Stephanie's brief message led.

And so, for planting the idea and supplying the motivation, I offer a tip of my hat to Michele and Michael and all my friends who have taken the time to respond to any of my online questions. I am ready to take the plunge.

It is my hope that this book will provide pleasure to those of you who already share my enthusiasm for theater and enjoy discovering how like-minded people think and feel about it. I hope, too, that this book will motivate theatrical novices to develop a greater interest in it, or perhaps to even get involved—as performers, as behind-the-scenes personnel, or as theatergoers, which is how all of us who are part of this book derive so many of the pleasures of life.

Chapter Two

WHO AM I, ANYWAY?

*S*o, who am I, anyway?

As I mentioned, I spent a great portion of my adult life teaching high school English. At one point—during my college years—I had thought about making theater my life's work, most likely as a press agent, but from a very early age, I knew I had another calling. And I couldn't have been happier than I was as the star of my own classroom for nearly three decades.

But theater was in my blood, though my fascination with it is totally mystifying to me. How, exactly, did I happen to turn into what is commonly referred to nowadays as a "theater geek"? I'll tell you . . . I don't know!

You see, I come from a long line of theatrical—what?—non-devotees, I suppose, would be the word. Nobody in my family had ever been involved in the theater, professionally or other-wise. Nobody in my family acted, or sang, or even sold refreshments during intermission. If I'm being completely honest, nobody in my family had ever had much interest in even going to SEE a play . . . and, for the most part, they still don't!

So, how this happened to me is anybody's guess.

Over the years, I have been heavily involved in theater, as an actor, usher, director, follow spot operator, playwright, lyricist, critic, producer, stage manager, theatrical archivist . . . you name it. Not bad considering I have never had a "real career" in the theater. Sure, I have been paid for some of my work—most often in the form of a stipend, a token, for what has added up to countless hours . . . no, years . . . of labor. Yes, labor. Perhaps nothing offers more pleasure than theater, on either side of the footlights, but I don't think anybody would ever say that being in the theater is easy . . . even on the level at which I have been involved, ranging from community theater to regional, with an occasional semi-professional tour thrown in. But theater, for me, has been strictly an avocation; no, it's been much more than that. It has become a veritable lifestyle, an obsession, if you will. It was through theater that I met some of my closest friends, only a handful of whom are involved professionally; felt moments of sheer terror and complete bliss while working on productions; and forged countless fond memories, many of which I happily share with you.

Theater has permeated every aspect of my existence. In my youth, my love of music was built not around the popular songs of the day but around original cast recordings of Broadway shows. Growing up, I had never taken a particular liking to writing . . . that is until I got to college and discovered that, if I wrote about them, I could see Broadway shows for free. I attended Queens College, part of the City University of New York, where, on my first day on campus, I made my way to the office of *Phoenix*, one of the student publications, and indicated a desire to become involved. Little could I have known that two years later I would become the paper's Arts Editor! Many years after that, the experience would afford me the opportunity to work as a freelance journalist for the *Queens Chronicle*, a weekly newspaper in my adopted home borough. Thanks to publisher **Mark Weidler** and editor-in-chief **Peter Mastrosimone**, I've had the pleasure of reporting on a wide variety of topics, including the local theater scene. And, in all my years of teaching, I found no better way to inspire students than by introducing them to the wonders of theater, often including plays in my curriculum and frequently taking classes on trips to see live performances.

Preparing this book brought back so many thoughts of the past, including a particular one that I hadn't had in years. While serving as Arts Editor of *Phoenix*, I had the idea to publish a weekly arts-related quiz. (Even all those years ago I must have had a thing for weekly questions!) One time it might have been about movies with numerals in their titles; another focused on television. And, of course, one aspect or another of Broadway was always in the mix. It was through one of those quizzes that I met one **Joseph Schneider**, whose winning category was movie debuts. He came to the newspaper office to collect his prize—a record album—and was disappointed that it wasn't one of **Barbra Streisand**'s. Our mutual love of Barbra—and the theater —led to a friendship that has lasted now for more than four decades.

I guess you could say theater most definitely changed my life. Perhaps it has already played a major role in yours, as well. Or maybe it will sometime in the future. I've become increasingly aware of how it has influenced so many of my friends, too. And, though they are scattered across the country—around the world, in fact, theater has, in a way uniquely unto itself, brought and kept so many of us together. And we enjoy expressing our opinions on it. Oh, yes, we sure do . . . as you will soon find out.

So, let's start at the very beginning . . .

(This might be as good a time as any to warn you: Like most lovers of musical theater, I tend to make a habit out of using words and phrases that have appeared in show tunes—unconsciously or otherwise—when I write and even more so when I speak. I would venture to guess that many of you might be guilty of doing the same. There have already been several instances up to this point. So, if you think you happen to catch some along the way while you're reading this, you're not imagining. In fact, you might enjoy trying to keep track of them. No advance peeking, but a complete list of all such references is to be found at the conclusion of the book. Until then, happy hunting!)

Chapter Three

HOW DID YOU BECOME HOOKED ON THE THEATER?

The first question I asked in the latest round was, "How did you become hooked on the theater?" which inspired some surprising revelations. I will reflect on my own response a bit later, but first I would like to share stories from some of my friends, who offered insight into the two main ways people first feel the passion: as participants or as members of the audience.

Emily Joyce, with whom I've worked on a few shows with the Free Synagogue of Flushing Community Theatre Group, or FSFCTG for short, in Queens, including *Hairspray* and an original revue, *The Magic of . . .* , a tribute to the various aspects of show business, said: "I did little kid theater starting when I was two, but I did an off-Broadway production of *The Most Happy Fella* when I was five and I got hooked on the rush of being out really late in rehearsal with people who loved making good theater. My mom actually put me in theater because I was marching around the house imitating **Margaret Hamilton** as The Witch, saying, 'You call that long?'"

It's not surprising that Emily first developed an interest in performing from having seen movies—including musicals—as a young child. Emily was obviously taken by *The Wizard of Oz*; who is there among us who has not been enchanted in one way or another by that film?

I must say a few words about FSFCTG. Of all the theater groups I've worked with, it was there that I did the most shows—more than two dozen over a period of about 25 years. Sadly, the group disbanded a few years ago, but **Maryellen Pierce**, its long-time artistic director, and some of its other members landed on their feet, founding a group that came to be known as Royal Star Theatre, which is happily alive and well.

Mitchell Kessler, whom I directed in several shows put on by the Patio Players: "In first grade, I played Barnaby in *Babes In Toyland*. School play in the gym. My entrance. Immediately, the cardboard mustache my mom made for me fell down to the floor. I picked it up. Roars of laughter surprised me. I put the mustache back. It fell again. Again laughter. Embarrassment came also with a big rush of power. My personal actions had a big impact on a crowd which was hanging on my every move. The acting bug infected me then and there."

[That's another aspect of the theater that provides endless fascination for me: things that go wrong on stage. See chapter 21 for some memorable recollections of these.]

Interestingly, the same show played a role in **Judith Mermelstein's** childhood, as well, or, I should say, she played a role in it, one that was to have a major influence on her future.

Judith, with whom I've never worked theatrically but whose children I taught and with whom I shared many a theatrical experience: "A camp production of *Babes In Toyland*. We were the youngest group, so young that I got the lead pretty much because I could read and memorize the lines and songs by myself! I was six."

TC Weiss, a fellow performer at Plaza Theatrical Productions, a prolific touring company on Long Island, run by **Kevin Harrington**, and my frequent navigator as we made our way to places unknown to me as we traveled: "I was one of the princes in *The King and I* for a fourth grade play. That's all it took. One step on the stage and I never left."

Shana Aborn, whom I first saw in a local Queens production of *Come Back, Little Sheba*, presented by the Parkside Players: "I guess it began in third grade when I was given the title role in a short play called *Clever Gretel*. I got laughs and applause and enjoyed it. I was in several school shows after that, but it was my eighth grade graduation that sealed the deal. We all did short sections from *Othello*, which we'd studied. I had one of Othello's monologues, and you could hear a pin drop in the auditorium as I performed. It was an unusually progressive school. In sixth grade, we did a socialist version of *Little Red Riding Hood*. In this version (in which I played Baby Bird #3), Red faces two nemeses: Wolf and Fox. She enlists her forest friends to ambush them by throwing pine cones and such. Then everyone sings a song to the tune of 'The Internationale.' I remember only a few scattered lyrics: 'The wolf is caught, the fox is caught/Victory is attained/Because we are friends!/We march boldly into battle/And now we're going home . . . The InterAnimale shall be a humane race!' Explains a lot about me, doesn't it?"

Of her performance in *Sheba,* I wrote in one of my earliest reviews in the *Chronicle*: "Lola (Shana Aborn) is an affection-starved housewife who, in this case, doesn't always get whatever she wants." Together with **Noel O'Neill,** as her alcoholic husband, Doc, I continued, "They evoke sympathy in the final moments, as the characters forgive each other and face the uncertain future together." And to think it all started with *Clever Gretel!*

Of course, seeing shows at an early age has left an indelible mark on many an impressionable future theater buff.

Bruce Bider, who has had a long career as a theater educator and director, primarily on Long Island, recalled: "My parents started taking me to see shows at Jones Beach and Westbury Music Fair at age seven. Then, the icing on the cake—for my eighth birthday—was seeing my first Broadway show, *No, No, Nanette,* with **Ruby Keeler**. That did it. My life's direction (passion?) was sealed that afternoon in the 46th Street Theatre."

Just a few words about those iconic venues. Jones Beach Theater, an outdoor amphitheater in Jones Beach State Park in Wantagh, Long Island, opened its doors in 1952 as the Jones Beach Marine Theater, with a seating capacity of about 8,200. For nearly 30 years, the stage was home to extremely lavish productions of Broadway musicals. In the 1980s, its focus changed, and concerts became the main attraction. Having undergone renovations in 1992, 2013 and 2017, the theater currently seats an estimated 15,000. But the kinds of shows that captivated so many theater-goers are, unfortunately, no longer on the bill.

As for Westbury Music Fair, a suburban theater-in-the-round on Long Island, it opened four years after the Jones Beach Theater, with ticket prices ranging from $2.50 to $4.50. It used to offer touring productions of many Broadway hits—both musicals and straight plays, though it is now known primarily as a concert venue. Having undergone multiple name changes, as well as renovations in both 1965 and 1992, it is known today as The NYCB (New York Community Bank) Theatre at Westbury.

The comments by Bruce inspired **Gary Tifeld**, who performs nearly non-stop on local stages, on Long Island and in Queens, to write, "My journey was very similar to **Bruce Bider**'s. I wanted to be a movie star, until my parents took me to see my first Broadway show, *No, No, Nanette*, for my eighth birthday. At one point, I thought Bruce and I might have been there at the same performance, but mine wasn't a matinee."

From **Debbie Vogel**, a long-time Broadway usher with whom I've never had the pleasure of working on a show but with whom I've developed a friendship via Facebook: "One of the highlights of my childhood was seeing musicals at Westbury Music Fair. My mom would play the record of the show many times before seeing it, so my sisters and I had memorized all the words. I loved performing in school shows. My sister, Laura, has an incredible voice, so I had the honor of seeing her in two Broadway shows, *Doonesbury* and *Tommy*. I performed a little as an adult, but found my niche working front of the house on Broadway. I see shows almost every night. The theater bug was passed down to my son, Stanford, and he is an active participant with The Gingerbread Players [of St. Luke's Church in Forest Hills, a section of Queens]. Theater is crucial to my life."

Ken Friedberg, another mainstay with the Patio Players: "My mom took me to see *The Sound of Music* with **Mary Martin**. It was magical. I still remember Ms. Martin singing, 'The hills are alive,' and saying to my mom, 'She's singing right to me!' It was an amazing afternoon. A few years later at summer camp, I played Kurt."

Tracey Berse Simon, a friend from my college days and a fellow reporter on *Phoenix*, put it this way: "My mom took my brother and me to see a Yiddish production called *A Cowboy Goes to Israel.* I was probably about five or six years old. I didn't understand a thing (my mom translated what she felt appropriate to translate), but it was just cool watching people in costumes doing weird things that piqued my interest. It also felt very grown-up to hand over a ticket and get a seat in a very fancy place. According to my mom, **Gertrude Berg** was sitting behind us and told my mother that she was doing a good job of translating for the 'kinder.' Why a woman as famous as Miss Berg would be sitting in the cheap seats was beyond me. But if the story was true, it added to the aura of being something special. To her it was true. She might have thought the woman was **Gertrude Berg**, but who's to say!"

Sadly, **Gertrude Berg** is all but forgotten today, but she was a true pioneer in her time. She was among the first women to create her own radio program, which premiered with a 15-minute episode on November 20, 1929. She played the role of Molly Goldberg, a character with whom she would become permanently identified. After 20 years on the radio, the show made its television debut, where it enjoyed further success.

So popular were the characters, in fact, that a musical based on them opened at the Alvin Theatre (now the Neil Simon) on Broadway in 1973, nearly half a century after they first appeared. It was called simply, *Molly*, and starred **Kaye Ballard** (or, rather, "Kay" Ballard, as this was during the time she had temporarily dropped the "e" in her name) in the title role. I saw it from the first row in the orchestra, having moved down from my assigned seat in row N, and, reviewing it in *Phoenix*, I said, "I wish I could offer 'Molly' a hearty welcome . . . the multi-talented Kay Ballard has been miscast . . . she is too loud and boisterous a performer . . . to play the soft-spoken Molly . . ." It's not likely that anyone could have been successful playing the role, though, as it was so closely associated with Miss Berg. Not a huge success, the show ran for 108 performances.

Some people seem to have found their way to the theater via rather circuitous routes. These include two friends I met while I was performing with Plaza.

Tommie Gibbons, director and choreographer: "As a freshman in high school, the chorus teacher told me I wouldn't have to serve detention if I did the musical *Annie Get Your Gun*. So, yeah."

Richard Allman, actor and technician: "I began with six years on a weekly musical radio show on CBS. When I moved to New York, it was only a short step to stage and T.V. My first show here was an off-Broadway thing called *One Fine Morning in the Middle of the Night*. As I recall, it lasted about four weeks."

Jack Taylor Macaluso, professional actor with whom I became acquainted on Facebook through our mutual friend, **Loria Parker**, who played a larger role in my love of theater than she could have ever imagined, more on which to come: "When I was very young, I saw a production of *Wait Until Dark* in Indonesia, where my family was living, in about 1966. I was taken over. It scared me shitless. Then we returned to the States and I was taken to New York City and saw *Funny Girl* and *Hello, Dolly!*

back to back. Hooked ever since. Can you believe I still have the Playbills?"

Interestingly, it was a production of *Wait Until Dark* in which I made what I consider to be my theatrical debut. Like most, I probably did some elementary school shows, though, I must confess, I don't have the slightest recollection of even a single one. I was in the chorus of my high school's SING competition in my senior year, but as far as I'm concerned, my life in the theater began in the Frederick Knott murder mystery, with The Paper Moon Players, a small community theater group in Brooklyn.

At the time, I was teaching at August Martin High School in Jamaica, a section of Queens, when I was approached by a colleague named **Bart Kaplan** about joining him in a play. From my involvement with my students in many theater projects he knew I had an interest but wasn't sure I had a desire to act.

It turned out I had! I drove nearly an hour on the infamously ever-jammed Belt Parkway to get to my audition at the church where the play would be performed. I read for the role of Patrolman Two, who makes his only appearance two pages before the final curtain—in total darkness:

"You better stay out of here, Mr. Hendrix!"

"Mr. Hendrix!"

"There's one of 'em. I'm going in there."

"There's a D.O.A. in there—looks like a knifing."

"Watch it!"

And that was it! Twenty-nine words! But I got the part! I was an actor!

THE
PAPER MOON
PLAYERS
PRESENT

FREDERICK KNOTT'S
WAIT UNTIL DARK

DIRECTED BY
RITA SHAPIRO

MAY 1985

The program from my theatrical debut.

WAIT UNTIL DARK
BY FREDERICK KNOTT

PRODUCED BY SPECIAL ARRANGEMENT WITH
DRAMATISTS PLAY SERVICE, INC.

CAST OF CHARACTERS
(In Order of Appearance)

Mike Talman	David Manchester
Sgt. Carlino	John Paine
Harry Roat	Marty Kelsohn
Susy Hendrix	Elissa Re
Sam Hendrix	Alyn Siegel
Gloria	Michele Brill
)	Leonard Burke
Policemen)	Bart Kaplan
)	Mark Lord

The action takes place in a basement apartment in Greenwich Village

ACT I

Scene 1: Friday Evening
Scene 2: Saturday afternoon
Scene 3: Twenty minutes later

ACT II

Scene 1: About an hour later
Scene 2: A few minutes later

DIRECTOR	Rita Shapiro
Stage Managers	Sherry Cohen
	Alan Schwartz
Set Design & Construction	Paper Moon Players
Graphic Art	Alyn Siegel
Publicity	Sherry Cohen
Lighting	Carol Gucci
Sound	Sherry Cohen
House Manager	Robin Weinstein

BIOGRAPHIES

MARK LORD (Policeman) Teaches English at August Martin High School, where he has directed and/or choreographed seven productions during the past five years. He conceived and wrote the title songs for two original pieces, Stay Tuned, based on popular TV shows, and Theater Magic, a compilation of theatrical scenes. He loves the theater and hopes this appearance, his first since high school, will lead to more acting assignments.

The first time my name appeared in a Cast of Characters listing.

You can imagine my devastation when in November of 2018 I got word that the scene of my official debut, the historic Emmanuel Episcopal Church, which dated to 1895, burned to the ground.

My earliest recollection of anything theatrical takes me back, as it did Jack, to a rather exotic place, or at least it was considered as such back in April of 1963. One night my parents took my brother and me to see a musical production in a community theater not too far from where we lived at the time—which happened to be, of all places, Puerto Rico.

How did that come to pass, you might well ask? I was born in Brooklyn, New York at a time when Puerto Rico was, in the minds of most Americans, an island floating in the middle of the world somewhere. When I was five years old, my dad, an accountant, got an offer to move there with the company for which he worked. My mom and dad talked it over and decided it would be a good opportunity for the entire family.

One night, my dad came home from work and told my mother that a co-worker, a woman named, as I recall, **Pauline Litwin**, offered him four tickets for a production of *The King and I*, which was to be performed at the Tapia Theatre, an historic landmark in Old San Juan.

Named after the Puerto Rican playwright **Alejandro Tapia y Rivera**, it officially opened its doors in 1832, and remains active until the present time, making it one of the oldest free-standing stages in the New World.

To my way of thinking, equally significant is the fact that it was in that building that my infatuation with the theater began.

Where it all began — The King and I *at the Tapia Theatre in Puerto Rico. The autograph came 10 years later at Damrosch Park in New York City.*

The tickets were for a weeknight and, to tell the truth, to this day I cannot believe that my mother would have agreed to let my older brother, Steven, and me stay out late when we had school the next day. My dad convinced her it was one night only and what would be the harm?

I was nine-and-a-half at the time and my life was about to be changed forever. We entered the theater and Steven, who has always been on the squeamish side, was immediately frightened by the art work depicted on the main curtain. I believe it was a projection of the masks of comedy and tragedy, though I couldn't vouch for that. All I know is, it scared Steven.

I, on the other hand, sat transfixed by all I saw and heard. I swear I can remember details of that show as if I had seen it last week. One line, in particular, struck me . . . most oddly. It came in an **Oscar Hammerstein II** lyric in the song, "Shall I Tell You What I Think of You?," which the schoolteacher, Anna, imagines addressing to The King. "How would you like it if you were a man playing the part of a toad?" she wondered aloud. It struck pre-pubescent me as curious that an actor, playing the part of a king, could, within that role, also portray, of all things, a toad. Of course, Anna meant it figuratively rather than literally, but I wasn't looking into it quite that deeply.

There were a few times, as I recall, that **Catherine Jacoby** (a name worth keeping in mind, as it will re-surface in a most delightful way later on), as Anna, seemed to open her mouth to sing but no words emerged.

I even asked Pauline about that after the show. Miss Jacoby, she explained, had been ill, and those moments of silence were remnants of vocal issues she had been suffering due to her illness.

How, I ask you, or why, would a nine-year-old even care about such things? I should have known then and there something was up.

[A sidebar about Pauline. Most of my life, I have thought of her and how her small but generous offer of those four comp tickets came to mean so much to me. I have a vague recollection of what she looked like. And I seem to recall that her parents owned a draperies company on the island. I have no idea how old she was at the time, or how old she might be today. I just wish there were some way of repaying her or at least letting her know how that show changed my world. As fate and my own tireless efforts would have it, there would be someone connected to the show to whom I would be able to express those precise feelings.]

And then there was the final scene in the play when (if you're reading this, I doubt the need of a spoiler alert) The King dies. I began to cry hysterically. My parents promised me that he really didn't die and that he would be coming out soon to take his curtain call. My consolation came only when I saw him once again, alive and well, and bowing at center stage.

I really don't recall how the show affected my parents, if at all, but Steven was pretty blase about his first theatrical experience. To this day he remains rather indifferent about going to the theater. I have often wondered to myself why I was so smitten. Was it that particular show that did it for me? Was I at a time in my life when any show I might have seen would have had the same effect? Had I first seen *The King and I* a few years later, would the results have been as dramatic? I'll never know, and, frankly, it really doesn't matter. I like to think it was just the right show at the right time—something that was meant to happen.

As anyone who knows me can attest, my feelings for *The King and I* have not diminished one iota since that evening more than 50 years ago. Throughout my life, the show has continuously brought me joy, and inspired me, and held special meaning for me on more occasions than I could count. In fact, as you will come to understand, it is a thread that weaves through my life —theatrical and otherwise.

Chapter Four

INTRODUCING YOUNG PEOPLE TO THEATER

*N*ot long ago, I was attending a performance of *Shrek The Musical* performed by The Gingerbread Players. I had never seen the show before and found it a complete delight. There was a young boy sitting alongside his mother, directly in front of me, who seemed to be having the time of his life. He sat in wide-eyed wonder as the actors came down the aisles, inches away from us, making their way to the stage. He was obviously drawn into the story, as every once in a while he would talk back to the characters as if they were part of his world. Well, actually, they were. Isn't that the magic of live theater?

Seeing this young boy's reactions made me think of my own first theatrical experience. After all these years, the feelings have never left me. I couldn't help but wonder, as I watched that little boy in front of me, if the show we were seeing would have the same lasting effect on him.

I figured he was about seven years old; his mother said he was actually five and this was his first full-length play, though he had seen other shorter ones in the past. His mother said she hadn't been sure if he would be able to sit so long and was very pleased when he proved that he could.

So, obviously *Shrek* is one show that might be recommended for introducing young people to theater. Several months ago, in fact, I had asked a question about this very topic: "What show would you recommend to introduce a young person to theater . . . and why?"

The responses were wide and varied, much more so than might have been anticipated. And, surprising even myself, I mentioned not the show I've already spoken about at length but another **Rodgers & Hammerstein** musical classic.

I wrote: "I guess most of you know that for me it was *The King and I*, but I might have to go with *The Sound of Music*. I think the story, the singable songs and the presence of children in central roles would all prove attractive to a young person."

Bruce Bider agreed with me: "Mine was *The Sound of Music* and I would suggest the same."

On a similar note, **Michele Gerrig Newmark** responded: "I would choose almost any **Rodgers & Hammerstein** musical. My sister was seven when we saw *The Sound of Music* during its pre-Broadway run. Ordinarily unable to sit still, she was motionless for the entire performance."

Naturally, several Disney-inspired musicals were mentioned.

Marilyn Garfinkel, whose father had been a mainstay of Queens theater before my time and who I've gotten to know—so far—only on Facebook: "The first show my kids saw was *Beauty and the Beast* and they loved it. They were each about eight when they saw it. They found it fun, so that's why I chose it. Great music, too."

Gary Eisele, a ubiquitous musical director who works all over Long Island, where we worked together on several Patio Players productions, took it from a performance perspective: *"The Little Mermaid.* Some songs are very singable. When I start to play the beginning of some songs, all the girls in rehearsal immediately shift gears and . . . sing along with me playing."

Brad Reiter, a former student of mine, started a bit of a debate: "I'd suggest something that was once a movie. *The Lion King* is something that kids are shown when they are young, and would be a great gateway show into live theater."

Tamara Derieux, whom I knew when we were children in Puerto Rico and with whom I reconnected on Facebook just a few years ago: "No, to *The Lion King* for a young child."

Tracey Berse Simon: "I would agree with *The Lion King*. They're familiar with the story and most of the songs."

There were some other controversial recommendations, as well.

Alison Feuer Pascuzzi, whom I first met in 1988 when she was Babe and I was Hines in the FSFCTG production of *The Pajama Game:* "I think *Oliver!* is a great introduction."

Marilyn Garfinkel: "I am not so sure about *Oliver!* The majority of scenes with Nancy and Bill Sykes are pretty scary for young ones i.m.h.o." [Far be it for me to clarify "modern" talk, but that would be "in my honest opinion."]

Debbie Vogel: "I totally agree. Bill Sykes is much too frightening for young children. It is a wonderful show, though."

Melanie Lee, an actress I directed in several shows, including a musical I wrote with **Joe Ferrante**, *Let's Hear It For Queens*, which premiered at the FSFCTG: "I saw the movie *Oliver!* when I was 11, and I didn't think the Bill and Nancy scenes were too scary for me. Of course, on stage, it may be different."

And then there were the pros and cons surrounding another classic.

Marilyn Garfinkel: "If we're talking adolescents, then I would say *West Side Story* because I think they would relate to this timeless story. And the songs!"

Melanie Lee: "I can easily see introducing kids of any age to the theater through *West Side Story*. The music, dancing and story are enthralling and I don't think the violence and death would be too much for little kids."

And yet another, this one surfacing rather late in the discussion, much to my surprise . . .

Marilyn Garfinkel: "I think *Annie* would be a great show to introduce kids to theater."

Julie Smith Smallman, with whom I shared the stage in a touring company called The Queens Jewish Theater, long defunct, and who I later directed in a production of the female version of *The Odd Couple* at the FSFCTG: "My only caveat for *Annie* would be that it's great for early double-digits, but younger kids might have trouble with the concepts of orphans and dead parents. You'd have to be ready to have a conversation about Mommy or Daddy dying and what would happen to them if they did."

Marilyn Garfinkel: "I can only go by my own experience with my kids. They both loved watching the film *Annie* when they were in single digits and neither thought to ask about dead parents."

And still one more . . .

Melanie Lee: "*1776* was the first show I remember seeing on Broadway. I was 14 or 15 and it was a trip for my high school class."

Robert Gold, with whom I've worked on many local productions, sharing the stage with him as well as directing him: "*1776* is a show I have done but in a cut version. It is way too long and too talky for an audience of kids today. They don't really have that good an attention span."

Miles Tepper, whom I've never met but with whom I've engaged in many a theater-related discussion online: "*1776* is really an adult show . . . though we could agree it's an entertaining way to introduce young people to American history. I was in a wonderful production of it in New York City back in the '80s. My wife's aunt cried at and after the signing of the Declaration, especially when the scrim came down and we froze, emulating the famous painting, and the signatures of the signers were projected on the scrim."

Jonathan Lapin, a friend since my childhood days in Puerto Rico whom I have not seen in about 50 years, set off an interesting discussion when he said: "I have to pick *The Music Man*. It's bright and refreshing and surprisingly seditious in its attitude towards the ruling class."

Miles Tepper: "I still find *The Music Man* just too corny, although I appreciate its construction and some of the songs are catchy."

I had to defend what is one of my top-ten favorite shows, one that I've been in three different times (twice as Mayor Shinn, once as Charlie Cowell, the anvil salesman) and directed on three other occasions.

I responded: "I think it's one of the most brilliant scores. Never mind that 'Rock Island' was the rap song of its time. Never mind that 'Trouble' is one of my all-time favorite patter songs. Never mind that there are three or four beautiful ballads. Never mind the songs given to the quartet. Never mind that several of the songs just flow effortlessly out of dialogue. Never mind . . . oh, never mind. I guess you can tell I love it!"

A variety of other shows were mentioned at least once, each recommended as a possible theatrical introduction.

Julie Smith Smallman: "*You're a Good Man, Charlie Brown.* They are familiar characters, nothing too intense."

Brad Reiter: "My first show was *The Phantom of the Opera,* and I loved it. That might be a little much. I was about eight or nine. My aunt knew someone who worked backstage, so we saw the show and then they gave us a tour behind the scenes."

Louise Guinther, a driving force with The Gingerbread Players: "*She Loves Me.* It's a perfect show. I would use it to introduce anyone of any age to theater."

Andrew Dinan, a long-time leading player with the same group: "For teens, *The Fantasticks.*"

Cheryl Cuddeback, who was in a local production of *Fiorello!* with me: "*Peter Pan*, so they won't grow up. Hee Hee."

Judith Mermelstein agreed with that one, though not necessarily for the same reason: "*Peter Pan* has a wonderfully singable score and great over-the-top characters, plus audience participation. And flying!"

Loria Parker (there's that name again!): "*Hamilton* because it's the music of their time and it's American history. Also, it's brilliantly performed. The music we grew up on in many cases is not what kids are listening to now."

Besides the specific shows that were named, several bits of general advice were also offered:

Tracey Berse Simon: "Start off with a high school production of a musical like *Bye Bye Birdie*. It's affordable, and the productions are usually well done."

Jacqueline Schnapp Schwartz, who played Mrs. Paroo to my Mayor Shinn in one of those *Music Man* productions: "Just give a child bright colors, singing and dancing, and they will be happy."

We'll give the last word on this to **Miles Tepper**, who took things in a totally different direction: "If we're not limited to musicals, the sky's the limit. My first show (at age 13) was *A Raisin In the Sun*, and I loved it—but more serious you cannot get."

Chapter Five

THE SUBJECT I LIKE MOST

*A*mong the more recent questions I posed was this one: What is one thing about theater that is frequently misunderstood, and how would you explain it?

As I put it, "I don't think the average theatergoer appreciates the amount of time and work that go into a show. Most people probably never stop to think about it, nor should they necessarily. I'd invite them to one rehearsal—that's all it would take for them to see what a complex undertaking theater is."

Here's what some of my friends had to say:

Matt Ian, a young Facebook friend whom I happened to run into once on the street in the neighborhood in which we both live and who is as obsessed with theater as I am: "The challenges of working front-of-house (box office, house management, ushering, concessions, etc.)"

Debbie Vogel: "Thank you for pointing that out. Sometimes there's more drama front-of-house than on stage, but the show goes on. Too many patrons show up late. Usually, it's someone in the middle of the row and someone else has decided to move to their seat or put their coat on the empty seat. The usher has to diplomatically try to get the late patron into the right seat. The on-time patrons often get annoyed that they're being inter-rupted. The seats are very narrow, so we often have to try to relocate patrons with long legs, who have recently had surgery, or who bought tickets in the mezzanine who can't do stairs (at a theater with no elevator). This is very tricky at a sold out show. Unfortunately, patrons are not always considerate of their fellow patrons or actors. They constantly talk during the show or are opening candy wrappers. Patrons also get sick during the show. When I was once escorting a patron to the restroom, she threw up all over me. Patrons also need emergency medical care and getting the paramedics into the theater while not disturbing the show is tricky. Front-of-house is the first means of support for patrons' safety and health during the show. The job is much more than helping patrons find their seats."

Marilyn Garfinkel: "The amount of time that goes into the show is often at the expense of the performers' families. I loved my dad and loved seeing him perform in many community theater performances. But I hated how often he had to go to rehearsals and not be at home."

Solomon Buchman, whom I directed in a couple of original musical revues for the Patio Players: "When I tell people that I also produce shows, as well as perform in them, many of them ask me what it is that I do in that capacity. I wasn't too sure either until I started doing it a few years ago. I tell them that the producer is, in some ways, like the general contractor on a construction job. He has to know all the tasks that must be accomplished in order for the show to go up, then makes sure he has the people and other resources needed to accomplish those tasks. And, finally, he has to make sure that everything is getting done on time and correctly. To that end, the producer's job is to make up plans, set them in motion, and then spend an obscene amount of time and energy putting out all the proverbial fires that spring up in opposition to those plans. That can be, and often is, nerve-racking."

Tracey Berse Simon: "How difficult it is to be an actor. Many people think it's just memorizing lines and saying them with feeling. They don't understand that an actor must find a way to 'inhabit' the person they are playing to make that character believable. Also, some folks forget that theater is like a movie in that you must have a 'willing suspension of disbelief.' It may be difficult for some to follow theater because they see it as live, therefore 'real.' My dad had this problem. We took him to see *Da* one Father's Day, and he couldn't understand how the son could talk with his dead father face to face. This may have explained why he enjoyed reading non-fiction over fiction."

Michael Brooks: "Stage management! Unequivocally!! It blows me away every show I'm in! It takes an extraordinary amount of time, patience, and attention to detail! That is why exceptionally talented people perform this job!"

Scott Haimes, one of the main "tekkies" at the Patio Players: "Definitely how much planning and engineering goes into a show. The lighting, the sound, the rigging, the logistics of making everything happen smoothly, the role of the stage management in coordinating all of these different things, the costumes, wigs, and make-up, the scenery, and everything coming together perfectly."

Russ Woolley, a producer extraordinaire, whom I met a couple of years ago, when I was hired to stage manage a series of cabaret shows in Manhattan: "I think one thing which is often misunderstood is that fans are entitled to get autographs at the stage door afterward. The only thing a fan should be ensured of is an actor or actress giving their best performance."

Jef Lawrence, a man with a long list of credits on the local scene whom, somehow, I've never worked with: "I find many non-theater people don't realize how many rehearsals there are and how many weeks (or months) it takes to put on a production. Some people just think you memorize the lines and practice a couple times."

And one friend of mine put the whole thing in a different perspective:

Andrew Dinan: "While I think it is important that people who are involved in theater appreciate what our peers do and the effort required to accomplish their roles, I don't think that is something we should be trying to make the audience under-stand. A good magician never reveals his tricks."

Chapter Six

MEETING "MRS. ANNA"

I think we would all agree that theater provides many of life's most gratifying moments. I'd like to share a very special one, one which took place exactly 10 years after I had seen *The King and I* as a child in Puerto Rico.

I picked up one of the daily New York newspapers (there must have been at least half a dozen at the time) and was thrilled when I read that a free performance of the show was going to be given at the Guggenheim Band Shell in Damrosch Park, right on the outskirts of Lincoln Center, the performing arts complex that houses the Metropolitan Opera, the New York City Ballet, the New York Philharmonic and other world-class institutions.

The outdoor amphitheater had been completed just four years earlier, so I found it a particularly exciting place to visit on a warm spring or summer evening, all the more so on one particular day, when my favorite show was going to be performed.

My amazement was amplified when, a few days later, I discovered that the cast would include several of the actors I had seen in Puerto Rico, recreating their respective roles, including **Raul Davila**, as The King, **Constance DiGiovanni** (who, by this time, went by **Constance Velero**) as Tuptim, **James Demas** as The Kralahome, and, most significantly to me, **Catherine Jacoby** as Anna. (I told you to keep that name in mind!)

```
                    "THE KING AND I"
             (A Rodgers & Hammerstein Musical)
                          Cast
                  (In order of appearance)

Captain Orton ......... CARLOS PEREIRA
Louis Leonowens ....... MARK FABLE (Aug. 29,30, Sept.3) - BOBBY PANCHERI -
                                               (August 31, Sept. 1,2)
Anna Leonowens ........ CATHERINE JACOBY
The Interpreter ....... RAMON CABALLERO
The Kralchome ......... JAMES DEMAS
The King ............. RAUL DAVILA
Phra Alack ........... RAUL BETANCOURT
Tuptim ............... CONSTANCE VELERO
Lady Thiang .......... PULI TORO
Prince Chulalongkorn ... MARCUS TICOTIN
Lun Tha .............. RAFAEL LE BRON
Sir Edward Ramsay ..... KIRK WILLIAMSON

Royal Princes and Princesses - GINA GARDINI, DANNY TICOTIN, TONY FABLE, LUISA
      GONZALES, KAREN ALEQUIN, JAY ALEQUIN, CRYSTAL SEPULVEDA, ALEX
      ALMENDAREZ, NAOMI TICOTIN, LAURIE DE LORENZO, ARTIE DE LORENZO.

Royal Wives - IDA MALDONADO, CLARA CABRERA, MILAGROS SANTIAGO, BERTA CARELA,
      MICHELLE BETETA, ELSIE MORALES, GEORGINA ROBLES, JUDITH GODOY,
      NILSA SANTIAGO, CYNTHIA RAMOS, LUZ CABRERA, LINDA LOPEZ,
      RUTH DIVIDSON

Priests and Guards - JOHN ALLER, ANDY DELGADO, ANDY FIGUEROA, MIKE GONZOLEZ,
      LUIS FLAHERTY, BENNY TORRES, RICHARD STOTTS, RICHARD CABRERA

The play is Divided into Two Acts.
The Action Passes in and Around the King's Palace,
Bangkok, Siam.
          Time: Early Eighteen Sixties
                 MUSICAL SYNOPSIS
                      ACT I
OVERTURE
 1. I Whistle a Happy Tune.....Anna & Louis
 2. My Lord & Master .........Tuptim
 3. Hello, Young Lovers........Anna & Wives
 4. The March of the Siamese Children
 5. A Puzzlement..............The King
 6. Getting to know you ......Anna & Wives,
                                    Children
 7. We Kiss In a Shadow .....Tuptim & Lun Tha
 8. Reprise: A Puzzlement...Prince & Louis
 9. Shall I tell you what I think of You..Anna
10. Something Wonderful .....Lady Thiang
11. Finale Act 1
                  INTERMISSION
                    Act 11
ENTR'ACT
 1. Western People Funny .....Lady Thiang & Wives
 2. I have Dreamed ..........Tuptim & Lun Tha
 3. Reprise: Hello Young Lovers ....Anna
 4. Small House of Uncle Tom....Tuptim and
                              Royal Dancers
 5. Shall We Dance ......Anna & the King
 6. Reprise: Something Wonderful
 7. Reprise: I Whistle a Happy Tune
 8. Finale Ultimo
```

* * * * *   * * * * * *   * *   * *

RAUL DAVILA, one of Puerto
Rico's outstanding stage and
television actors, is re-
creating the role of the King,
which he played in the Robert
Cox production several years
ago in Puerto Rico. CATHERINE
JACOBY, CONSTANCE VELERO,
JAMES DEMAS, and RAMON
CABALLERO were also in the
previous production in San
Juan are happily reunited
for the current show.

* *   *   * * * * * *   * * *

We would like to dedicate
THE KING AND I to JEAN
DALRYMPLE, who produced so
many lovely musicals of THE
KING AND I inspired us to
present it in the first
place. Thank you, Miss
Dalrymple ... we miss those
wonderful musical theatre
seasons at City Center and
hope they will one day be
revived!!!

* * * * * * * * * * * * * *

The program from the Damrosch Park production of The King and I, *ten years after the Tapia Theatre production.*

The day of the performance finally arrived and I took the subway into Manhattan. I could scarcely contain my excitement. Naturally, I was looking forward to seeing the show, but it was the possibility of meeting the actors afterward, and sharing with them all that their earlier performance had meant to me, that I found most exciting.

So fixated was I on the idea of coming face to face with the actors that the actual performance is entirely a blur.

After the curtain calls, I dashed over to the stage entrance, and the cast began to emerge. Someone connected to the show asked me who I was waiting for and I said I particularly wanted to meet Mr. Davila and Miss Jacoby.

Mr. Davila, I was told, had already taken his leave, apparently through another exit, but I was assured that Miss Jacoby would be coming out shortly.

A few minutes passed and there she was. I walked up to her and said, "There's something I've been waiting 10 years to ask you."

She gave me an understandably quizzical look and asked, "Oh, what's that?"

I took out from behind my back the slightly stained program from the very production that had started me on my theatrical obsessions so many years before, extended it to her, and asked, "Would you please sign this for me?"

When she saw what I held in my hands, she looked like she was about to swoon. Who could blame her if she had, seeing a relic like that from so long ago and so far away?

With a thin-tipped green magic marker, she inscribed on the cover, "To Mark, Best wishes for the next 10 years & always, Cathy Jacoby."

"The next 10 years."

"The next 10 years."

It was a phrase that struck a chord in me. How cool would it be, I thought to myself, if we could somehow catch up with each other every 10 years? You know, sort of like what happens in the *Up* documentaries, a series of films that, every seven years, offers an update on the lives of its 14 protagonists, British citizens who were included in the longitudinal study since they were seven years old.

Of course, when I met Cathy that day in the park it was long before the world ever even dreamed of Facebook, which would have made keeping in touch so very simple.

But simple doesn't always translate to special.

Over the years, I had kept the idea in mind, but would I really ever be able to get in touch with her again?

Chapter Seven

MY TWO WORLDS COME TOGETHER

ollowing graduation from Queens College in 1975, I hoped to find a position as an English teacher at a high school somewhere in Queens, but New York City was facing a financial crisis at the time and a hiring freeze was in effect. But within five weeks, I was lucky to find a job working in a small publishing company, where I would remain for the next several years.

I finally received an appointment to August Martin High School in the fall of 1980. The way that came about is a story unto itself, perhaps for another time. What matters is that the first day I reported for work, I approached my department chairperson: Do you do plays in this school?

She gave me one of those "are you kidding?" looks and said, "We haven't had a play in years.""When I asked her why, she said none of the teachers were interested in getting involved. I said I was.

She suggested I meet my classes and settle in first and then we could talk about it again. Thus, my career as a director was about to get under way.

How I had the nerve to think I could direct a play remains a mystery to me. Chalk it up to innocence and the enthusiasm of youth, I guess. I had never directed a play before; in fact, I had never really been involved in a production in any capacity, except possibly in elementary school, though I can't remember for sure. And that would have been a long, long time before.

A short time passed and I raised the subject again with my chairperson. She suggested I see **Rosemarie Castanza**, the chairperson of the department of music and art. I would recognize her, she said, by the bun in her hair. I found my way to her office. There she was, her trademark coiffure firmly in place.

I introduced myself, explaining I was a new teacher and interested in directing a school play. She seemed open to the idea and asked if I had any particular show in mind.

"I was thinking about *The King and I*," I told her.

"That's quite an ambitious show," she replied. But she agreed we could give it a shot.

She had already been in the school for years and knew many of the students, especially anyone with musical talent. They always seemed to gravitate toward her.

We scheduled auditions and had quite a decent turnout, as I recall. I was very impressed by the talent. "This is going to be a cinch," I thought to myself. The two of us went off to discuss casting.

I suggested a particular student, a young man with a beautiful singing voice, for a certain role and Rosemarie shook her head.

"Not reliable," she warned.

Okay. How about . . .

And so we went down the list, trying to match actors to roles, while keeping in mind any other such circumstances that were extraneous to the actual production.

We managed to assemble a cast—quite an outstanding one, in fact. Our leading lady, **Susan Giles**, was the real deal: talented, serious about her craft, mature beyond her years. She was an elegant, intelligent Anna, and even captured the English accent that gave her performance its special appeal. She would go on to carve out a musical career for herself, still performing these days as a jazz singer. As The King, **Michael Bryant** had a wonderful presence and fine singing voice, and the two had terrific chemistry . . . yes, chemistry!

Our Lady Thiang, **Marilyn Buchanan**, had a beautiful voice and held a note in her solo so long that it brought cheers every time she sang it. And she also had a wicked sense of humor. During one rehearsal, when Anna asked her, "Why do you call me 'sir'?" a term The King's head wife used out of respect, instead of responding with the scripted line, "Because you scientific. Not lowly, like woman," she replied, "Because you manly." The entire cast broke up, of course, and, to tell you the truth, so did I. Actually, our Anna was as ladylike as could be.

Derrick Johnson, the young man playing Prince Chulalongkorn, had a wonderful personality and he lit up the stage in each appearance. But he spoke with an unmistakable New Yorkese that was not at all appropriate for the role. Try as we might to at least temporarily break him of the accent, we never did. I can hear his line deliveries to this day. Concerned about his father's health, he asked Lady Thiang, "Motha, what is it with my fatha?" He was most decidedly not his mother's son!

And then there was **Stuart Brewton**, the fresh-faced freshman who played Anna's son, Louis. He must have been barely five feet tall at the time, and somewhere along the way I began to refer to him as "Little Louis." I'm still in touch with him, and though he is now a foot taller, I still call him by his old nickname.

Opening scene from the August Martin High School production of The King and I, *featuring "Little Louis," Stuart Brewton, clutching the hand of Susan Giles as his mother, Anna.*

The production was met with incredible enthusiasm. It would be the first of about a dozen shows I would direct during my 14 years at the school. While one or two of the others came close, none ever quite matched that first endeavor.

There is a theater in Flushing Meadows Corona Park (in Queens, site of the 1939 and 1964 World's Fairs) that used to be known, appropriately, as Theater in the Park (its name has since evolved into Queens Theatre). It is a real jewel, a mini-Broadway theater. The year we did *The King and I,* the theater hosted a festival—a competition, actually—for the local high schools, inviting each to put on, for one night only, their respective school plays.

The night we were on, a group of adults with special needs was among the spectators. During one scene, set in The King's study, he is found comfortably reclining on the floor, reading an over-sized book, when Anna enters.

"Your Majesty is reading *The Bible!*" she says.

Before The King had a chance to respond, a woman in the audience did.

"I am *The Bible,*" she said. And she repeated the phrase—in a stage voice that many trained actors would have envied—two or three times. I was backstage and couldn't quite hear what was going on, but I heard a commotion and knew something was amiss.

I sized up the situation and my only thought was, "Thank God it was just the two leads on stage at the time." Had it been the entire cast, someone would have most assuredly reacted inappropriately. But I had confidence they would handle themselves like the total pros they were. And they did.

The festival ran for two weeks, with a dozen or so schools participating. At the conclusion of the festival, one production was selected as the most outstanding entry. Nearly 40 years later, I am still proud that our show won.

We received a large silver cup acknowledging our success. It was placed in the principal's office where, for years, I would stop by from time to time to visit it.

Rosemarie Castanza and I, surrounded by some cast members of The King and I, *proudly holding the silver cup we won for our production at Theater in the Park.*

I eventually transferred to another school and always wondered what might have happened to that cup. Would it still be on display or would a subsequent principal have decided it was nothing but a dust collector and tossed it into the trash can?

Fifteen years after I left Martin, I was planning my retirement from teaching. I mentioned the cup to my principal at the time, along with the story behind it, hoping he would take the hint and perhaps reach out to his counterpart at Martin about it, and, possibly, surprise me with it as a parting gift. Alas, it never happened.

Some years later, I heard rumors that Martin was going to undergo major changes, including its name. In the transition, I was convinced that the cup, if it were still there, would not survive and decided to try to retrieve it myself.

I returned to the school, made my way into the principal's office, and looked everywhere, but it was nowhere in sight. I asked as to its whereabouts, but no one seemed to know. No one even remembered that it had ever been there at all. But I did. And I do.

The finale of Act I of The King and I *at August Martin High School.*

The whole experience remains one of the highlights of both my teaching and theatrical careers.

Years later, Rosemarie and I were talking about the old days when she made a confession to me.

"Remember the day you came down to see me for the first time and you said you wanted to do *The King and I*?" she asked.

"Sure."

"To tell you the truth, I never thought we could pull it off, but you had such enthusiasm, I didn't have the heart to say no."

Chapter Eight

STAGE FRIGHT

a s a teacher, I often had nightmares—and still do even though I've been retired for years—about neglecting to take careful attendance, a "sin" I think I committed a grand total of once over my 29-year career. As a performer, I don't think I ever experienced the "actor's nightmare," being on stage unable to remember one's lines. But, in reality, I have suffered a great deal from stage fright. When I first began my onstage "career," I used to have major bouts of it. As the years went by, it became less and less of a factor, but it has never disappeared completely. I envy those who don't seem to suffer from it. **Ethel Merman** is known to have said that she never did, believing if anyone could do what she did as well as she, they'd be on stage and she'd be in the audience watching them! But many other equally stellar performers—among them **Barbra Streisand** and **Lord Laurence Olivier**—are on record as having suffered terribly from stage fright. I usually worry most about forgetting a line or a lyric. So, the best solution I've come up with is to know my lines like I know my name. The more sure I am, the less I'm affected by stage fright.

The funny thing is, the size of an audience, which seems to bother some people, has never really mattered to me. In fact, I sometimes feel more at ease in front of a huge crowd (10,000, I think, when we did *The Music Man* at a park on Long Island) than in front of 20 people in a church basement.

Waiting to go on in that Brooklyn production of *Wait Until Dark*, I would pace backstage every night, hearing the arriving audience chattering in their seats, and a sweat would come over me as panic began to wreak havoc on me. For two-and-a-half hours, I waited each night for my cue, for my chance to deliver my five lines—in pitch blackness. At times, my nerves were unbearable.

"They're not even going to see you," I kept reminding myself. That thought provided scant consolation.

With this in mind, I recently posed this question: "Those of you who perform, how do you deal with stage fright?"

Jef Lawrence: "I don't really get stage fright. But I think the ability to improv certainly helps. I've even changed song lyrics when I've forgotten them, but at least they still rhymed. I would recommend taking improv classes for anyone who suffers from stage fright."

Marilyn Garfinkel: "I've never been a stage actor, but I was a teacher at a blood bank for much of my career. The audience could be easily over 1,000 people. Training would take place in a large auditorium with a stage and I would teach from that stage. I must say I loved it. The more the merrier. I'm never frightened."

Mitchell Kessler: "Staying in character is important . . . I tell myself, 'The heck with the audience. I'm here to have fun. I'm good at this. I've been perfecting this for months and they're lucky that they get to watch!' It's kind of BS, but it helps!"

Judith Mermelstein: "I've learned how to use jitters to infuse energy into my performance. I've played before 50 people in a cabaret setting, 30 people in a coffee house, 100 people at a private party, and 5,000 people in Damrosch Park at Lincoln Center. I'm one of those very lucky people who've never been afraid of public speaking. Being very prepared helps, experience helps, but the most helpful thing is just being an unapologetic show-off."

Tracey Berse Simon: "When doing stand-up, I remind myself that I'm the one holding the microphone, the talisman of power. For actors, it can be, 'I'm the one on stage.' And as I learned from reading Torah at my adult Bat Mitzvah, there will always be one old man in the congregation—or for an actor, one theater geek— who will know all the words and will know when you've missed one. They are NOT the ones you are performing for. The ones who come to enjoy themselves and be entertained are."

Alice Goldman Kasten, who worked primarily behind the scenes at Theatre a la Carte, a now-defunct community theater group in Douglaston, Queens, where I made my musical theater debut as Senex, the dirty old man, in a production of *A Funny Thing Happened On the Way to the Forum*: "Teacher and presenter in front of groups large and small for over 50 years. Know your stuff. I was always more nervous in front of a small school board than in front of a huge convention auditorium. But I found if I knew what I was going to say/do, the nervousness went away as soon as I opened my mouth."

Andrew Dinan: "I try to take the same advice I got for interview and audition jitters. You have one opportunity to show what you can do and the people you are doing it for are hoping you will do it very well."

Mitchell Kessler: "When the first mistake [on stage] happens, whether it's mine or someone else's, that helps with stage fright. I feel—okay, it won't be perfect anyway, so the pressure's off. Now you can relax, and being relaxed usually prevents mistakes."

["That is so true," I responded. "Like purposely putting a tiny scratch on a new car."]

Ann Kittredge, a professional singer with whom I've worked on several shows: "I chant. It helps me to focus my efforts on the audience rather than myself."

Nana Bendana, with whom I've shared more stage time than just about anybody: "I've never really had stage fright. I think teaching helped because we were always 'onstage' in the classroom."

[To this comment, I replied, "You know, there were times when I had 'stage fright' in front of my own class. Luckily, it was just for a short period of time. Then it seemed to pass."]

Nana, formerly known as **Debbie Richardson**, and I appeared together in around a dozen shows. My hands were always freezing and her neck was always burning hot before making our first appearances. I used to cool her off and she used to warm me up. That takes collaboration to new heights, I would say!

Lloyd Baum, a frequent performer on stages in Queens and Long Island: "I get nervous before I get on stage, but that first step usually calms me down. The worst time I've ever had was as the second yeoman in *The Yeomen of the Guard.* I had to lead the yeomen on stage and had the first solo after the entire chorus sings. As I was standing in the wings, all of a sudden, in a total reverse, I had no problem remembering the lyrics, but the melody I had to sing completely left my head. Luckily, it came back as soon as I stepped into the light."

[The mind works in mysterious ways, doesn't it? I remember reading about an incident involving **Constance Towers** when she was appearing as Anna opposite **Yul Brynner** in the revival of *The King and I* that I got to see on Broadway. As I recall, she had already been doing the show for many, many months, singing, among other songs, "I Whistle a Happy Tune." One night, for who knows what reason, her mind was playing tricks on her and she sang, "I Whistle a Happy Song." As luck (or lack thereof) would have it, the show's composer, **Richard Rodgers,** happened to be in the audience that night.

He greeted her backstage after the show: "Song?"

"I couldn't think of the word 'tune,'" Miss Towers is said to have replied.]

Joe Riley, one of my oldest friends in the community theater circle: "I've always had stage fright. I have learned to embrace it. Rather than viewing it as an adversary, I see it more like a companion along for the ride, pumping adrenaline, heightening my senses, and keeping me sharp. The more I am able to lose myself in the role, the more manageable it becomes."

Renee Colavito, a fellow performing arts teacher who also performs: "If you don't feel any kind of stage fright or even just some nervous energy, then you must be dead. (lol) I just trick myself into thinking that I'm not nervous. I'm just excited. I feel it in the wings, but once we're off and running, I'm in the mode. I forget about it."

Stu Freeman, whom I've known since my early days with The Paper Moon Players: "I deal with stage fright by considering how humiliated I'll be if I really do blow my lines."

Chapter Nine

A "TYPICAL" DAY WITH HAROLD PRINCE

*T*houghts of stage fright and blowing lines reminded me of an incident that happened about 20 years ago, when I met **Harold Prince** for the second time in my life.

The first encounter took place during my college days. I, of course, had already had a long-standing love affair with the theater, and I have always enjoyed being around show people. I would take advantage of every opportunity to be in their company. **Harold Prince** had long been an idol of mine, having already had an incredible career by that time, with credits as director and/or producer that included *Fiddler On the Roof, Company, The Pajama Game, Damn Yankees, West Side Story, A Little Night Music, A Funny Thing Happened On the Way to the Forum, Follies, Cabaret* and on and on. Of course, he would go on to direct his greatest success, *The Phantom of the Opera*, years later. At one point, he found time to direct plays for The New Phoenix Repertory Company.

The company, it is worth noting, had a long, complicated existence. It was a pioneer of the off-Broadway scene, founded in 1953, and originally located at 12th Street and Second Avenue. It later moved to East 74th Street, and eventually to Broadway's Lyceum Theatre, before taking a more nomadic approach. Near the end of its third decade, it settled into the basement of St. Peter's Evangelical Lutheran Church, but financial woes soon did it in and, in 1982, it ceased operation. That final venue is now home to the York Theatre.

During its 30 years, Phoenix was not only—on and off—a repertory company, but, at one point, it even merged with another company, the Association of Producing Artists for a while, a pairing that called itself the APA-Phoenix Theatre or the APA-Phoenix Repertory Company.

As one of the founders of the New Phoenix company, Mr. Prince directed several shows within a short period of time, and, to be honest, I can no longer remember through which one it was that I had the opportunity to meet him. I was fortunate to have been allowed to sit in on the first day of rehearsal of one of the plays, thanks to the efforts of his press agent, **Mary Bryant**, with whom I had developed a wonderful relationship while reviewing shows for the Queens College *Phoenix* (no connection to the rep company). It was also Mary who placed an ad in the paper shortly after I reviewed *A Little Night Music*. To my delight she included a line from my review—the first time I had ever been so quoted.

I should also mention that I wrote two articles about Mary and her work, partially because I thought my readers would be interested, and—confession time—because I was, at that point, strongly considering becoming a press agent, and I wanted to learn all I could about the profession.

The first time I was quoted in an ad for a show.

As Mary explained it, a press agent's primary job is to arrange all publicity for a show—anything that is not paid for. "It's a strange business," I quoted her as saying. "You could be sitting there with no shows and the phone rings and you have a show. If someone is talented in this business, they get the business." She admitted that luck also features in an agent's success.

In addition to Mary, I interviewed two other press agents, **Sandra Manley** and **Joshua Ellis**, with whom I am in contact on occasion on Facebook. Josh told me at the time about his belief that theater is special. As for his job, he couldn't imagine people not wanting to do it. And now, all these years later, he is apparently still as much in love with theater as ever.

But I digress, as I am wont to do! At some point while I sat in on the rehearsal, Mr. Prince came over to introduce himself (as if that was really necessary!) and welcome me. I was maybe 19 or 20 at the time, and chatted with this Broadway legend as if we were old friends. Pretty heady stuff for a college kid, don't you think?

Fast forward some 25 years. I was attending a performance of the new **Charles Busch** play, *The Tale of the Allergist's Wife*, then being performed on Stage 2 at Manhattan Theatre Club, prior to its Broadway transfer. It's an intimate space and from my seat near the door I could see everyone who entered the theater. Shortly before the lights dimmed, in walked Mr. Prince himself. I think I was more excited about seeing him than the show. And, lo and behold, where does he sit? Directly in back of me! I must admit I had a difficult time concentrating on the play. All I could think about was whether or not I should approach him at intermission. I was dying to remind him of the time we had met previously, which I'm sure hadn't made as big an impression on him as it had on me. I decided to leave the man alone. But fate—and his interest in what I did during the play—would ultimately lead us to our second conversation.

The Manhattan Theatre Club had offered teachers wonderful opportunities to see their plays, along with participatory workshops a few days prior. We were sent copies of the scripts in advance to help us prepare for the workshops, which would include discussions of the plays and various interactive activities with their teaching artists.

So, by the time I saw *Allergist's Wife* I was already familiar with the play. As I sat in the theater, waiting for it to begin, an idea popped into my head. As a community theater actor, I don't think I've ever been involved in a production in which we got every line of dialogue exactly right. And I wondered if professional actors were actually able to accomplish that during a performance. I had my copy of the script with me, having just come from the workshop, and I decided to take it out and follow along as I watched the play.

The cast, I should point out, was stellar: **Linda Lavin**, who gave an absolutely wonderful performance, receiving a Tony Award nomination for the show's Broadway incarnation; **Michele Lee**, who I had loved since seeing her in *Seesaw* so many years before; **Tony Roberts**, a veteran of countless plays and musicals; and two actors who were new to me at the time, **Shirl Bernheim**, who I later discovered was living in my neighborhood, and **Anil Kumar**, who would ultimately make his Broadway debut in this play.

Had I not had the script on hand, I would never have noticed anything was amiss during the performance, BUT . . .

While the other actors pretty much nailed their lines, Miss Lavin had a tendency to paraphrase hers, most likely to the dismay of the rest of the cast but certainly not to the detriment of the play. In fact, I thought she was the best part of it.

Having proven to myself that even pros don't necessarily stick precisely to a script, I put my copy away and watched act two like a "normal person."

After the show, I wanted to meet Miss Lee and tell her how much I had enjoyed her work through the years. As I stood outside the stage door, I heard a voice from the other side say something like, "And there was a man sitting in front of me . . . " That was all I could make out. But I had the feeling the voice belonged to Mr. Prince, and I suspected he was talking about me. With that, the door opened; there stood Mr. Prince, in mid-conversation with Miss Lavin herself! As he saw me, he said to her, "That's him!"

I don't know who was more panicky, Miss Lavin or myself. I wondered if I had broken some cardinal rule of theater by doing what I had done. She became noticeably agitated and, in a single breath, said, "You have a copy of the script? How could you have a copy of the script? It hasn't even been published yet." I explained how I had come to have it and that seemed to comfort her. She signed my Playbill (had I thought of it, I would have asked her to sign the script, too!), bid Mr. Prince and me adieu, and took off.

So, there I was outside the stage door, alone with Mr. Prince, our first face-to-face encounter in some two decades. "I want to thank you," I said to him, "for something you did 20 years ago."

"Oh, what was that?" he asked.

I reminded him of our earlier meeting and how kindly he had treated me that day at rehearsal. He seemed pleased that it was such a fond memory for me.

And then he said, "May I ask you a question?"

"Sure," I said, suspecting what was coming.

"Why were you following along with the script?"

"I do community theater," I explained, "and we never seem to be able to get it just right. I wanted to see how the pros do."

"And how did they do?" he asked.

I took a deep breath and, without offering specifics, said, "Well, actually not too well."

"Typical!" he replied.

———————

Prince's passing on July 31, 2019, just as this book was about to go to publication, created a deep void in the entire theater community, one which will likely never be filled. Following tradition, the lights were dimmed at every Broadway theater in his honor. I felt the loss as I might feel the loss of a personal friend.

Chapter Ten

IT'S TIME FOR A TOP-TEN LIST!

The January 26, 2018 question was simple to ask but perhaps difficult to answer: What musicals would make your Top-Ten list?

My choices have evolved, slightly, over time, but the majority have remained constant. In the time-honored way of the theater —alphabetical order—here are my picks:

- *Cabaret*
- *Fiddler On the Roof*
- *Fiorello!*
- *A Funny Thing Happened On the Way to the Forum*
- *The King and I*
- *The Music Man*
- *My Fair Lady*
- *Ragtime*
- *The Sound of Music*
- *West Side Story*

It's interesting, I think, that the most recent show on my list, *Ragtime,* opened some 20 years ago. Call me a cockeyed optimist, but I have to believe that just around the corner somewhere is an even newer show waiting to knock one of my top picks off the list, though I can't imagine which one I would ever be able to drop.

Understandably, the selections have a lot to do with the age of the person responding, with younger "voters" tending to elect more recent shows. I hope that, as younger people read through this book, and these lists, in particular, they will feel motivated to check out at least some of the titles that appear over and over. Of course, the same holds true for us older folks. I, personally, hope to expose myself to some more recent musical works. I keep hearing there is lots of new talent creating shows for the musical theater, and I certainly wouldn't want to miss out on anything.

So, here's how 24 of my friends, from all walks of my life, responded to this "survey," with most indicating that their choices were listed in no particular order. Understandable, isn't it? I have taken the liberty of alphabetizing all of the titles on each list, which I don't think would bother any of them.

On the following pages are the results. A tally and brief analysis are included because . . . well, I thought they should be. Enjoy!

MARILYN GARFINKEL:

- *Cabaret*
- *Carousel*
- *Fiddler On the Roof*
- *Guys and Dolls*
- *Man of La Mancha*

- *The Music Man*
- *Oklahoma!*
- *The Sound of Music*
- *South Pacific*
- *West Side Story*

EMILY JOYCE:

- *Dear Evan Hansen*
- *Fun Home*
- *Guys and Dolls*
- *Into the Woods*
- *La Cage Aux Folles*
- *The Last 5 Years*
- *Rent*
- *The 25th Annual Putnam County Spelling Bee*
- *Urinetown*
- *The Wedding Singer*

Emily, I should point out, added that we might try asking her the same question again a few weeks later, as her list is always changing. A lot of us, I'm sure, could relate.

The next two lists share not a single title but, instead, have something else in common: some rather esoteric selections.

EDWARD SANTOS:

- *Applause*
- *Bounce*
- *Coco*
- *Dear World*
- *Follies*

- *Honeymoon In Vegas*
- *Legs Diamond*
- *Mame*
- *No, No, Nanette*
- *Sweeney Todd*

GARY EISELE:

- *Dracula, the Musical*
- *The Education of H*Y*M*A*N K*A*P*L*A*N*
- *Fiddler On the Roof*
- *Flora, the Red Menace*
- *A Funny Thing Happened On the Way to the Forum*
- *Guys and Dolls*
- *Li'l Abner*
- *Oklahoma!*
- *South Pacific*
- *West Side Story*

BRUCE BIDER:

- *Flower Drum Song*
- *George M!*
- *Guys and Dolls*
- *Hello, Dolly!*
- *Milk and Honey*
- *The Most Happy Fella*
- *The Music Man*
- *My Fair Lady*
- *Oklahoma!*
- *Show Boat*

DEBBIE VOGEL:

- *Camelot*
- *Carousel*
- *Come From Away*
- *Dear World*
- *Gypsy*
- *The King and I*
- *The Lion King*
- *My Fair Lady*
- *Show Boat*
- *West Side Story*

ALICE GOLDMAN KASTEN:

- *Carousel*
- *City of Angels*
- *Fiddler On the Roof*
- *Fiorello!*
- *A Funny Thing Happened On the Way to the Forum*
- *Guys and Dolls*
- *Gypsy*
- *Into the Woods*
- *Ragtime*
- *Sweeney Todd*

ERIN CLANCY BALSAMO:

- *Carousel*
- *Fifty Million Frenchmen*
- *Fiorello!*
- *Groundhog Day*
- *Hamilton*
- *Into the Woods*
- *Jesus Christ Superstar*
- *The Lion King*
- *Pippin*
- *Sweeney Todd*

DONALD GORMANLY:

- *Avenue Q*
- *Elegies: A Song Cycle*
- *Falsettos*
- *Groundhog Day*
- *Jesus Christ Superstar*
- *Les Miserables*
- *Little Shop of Horrors*
- *The Music Man*
- *SpongeBob SquarePants*
- *The 25th Annual Putnam County Spelling Bee*

EDWARD SIGALL:

- *Evita*
- *Guys and Dolls*
- *The King and I*
- *Les Miserables*
- *The Lion King*
- *Little Shop of Horrors*
- *The Phantom of the Opera*
- *Spamalot*
- *West Side Story*
- *Wicked*

MICHAEL BROOKS:

- *Fiddler On the Roof*
- *A Funny Thing Happened On the Way to the Forum*
- *Guys and Dolls*
- *The King and I*
- *Les Miserables*
- *Miss Saigon*
- *The Music Man*
- *The Phantom of the Opera*
- *South Pacific*
- *West Side Story*

BILL LOGAN:

- *Candide*
- *Company*
- *Gypsy*
- *Hello, Dolly!*
- *Nine*
- *Ragtime*
- *She Loves Me*
- *Show Boat*
- *Sweeney Todd*
- *West Side Story*

MEG MICHEELS:

- *Annie Get Your Gun*
- *Cabaret*
- *Gypsy*
- *The Last 5 Years*
- *Little Shop of Horrors*
- *The Music Man*
- *Newsies*
- *The Pajama Game*
- *Songs for a New World*
- *West Side Story*

STEPHAN:

- *Follies*
- *Hello, Dolly!*
- *The King and I*
- *A Little Night Music*
- *The Music Man*
- *My Fair Lady*
- *The Roar of the Greasepaint, The Smell of the Crowd*
- *The Rothschilds*
- *Show Boat*
- *Something Rotten*

MICHELE GERRIG NEWMARK:

- *Carousel*
- *Fiorello!*
- *The King and I*
- *The Music Man*
- *Oliver!*
- *Ragtime*
- *She Loves Me*
- *The Sound of Music*
- *Sunday in the Park with George*
- *Sweeney Todd*

DANA JAFFE:

- *Ain't Misbehavin'*
- *Chicago*
- *A Chorus Line*
- *Fiddler On the Roof*
- *Follies*
- *A Funny Thing Happened On the Way to the Forum*
- *Gypsy*
- *Nine*
- *Once On This Island*
- *West Side Story*

JK LARKIN:

- *Assassins*
- *Big Fish*
- *Come From Away*
- *Dear Evan Hansen*
- *Falsettos*
- *Fiddler On the Roof*
- *Groundhog Day*
- *Hamilton*
- *Pippin*
- *[title of show]*

CANDEE SHEPPARD:

- *The Fantasticks*
- *Follies*
- *Into the Woods*
- *Joseph and the Amazing Technicolor Dreamcoat*
- *The King and I*
- *Man of La Mancha*
- *Rent*
- *She Loves Me*
- *South Pacific*
- *West Side Story*

JOE RILEY:

- *A Funny Thing Happened On the Way to the Forum*
- *Guys and Dolls*
- *Gypsy*
- *Jesus Christ Superstar*
- *The King and I*
- *Les Miserables*
- *Little Shop of Horrors*
- *Man of La Mancha*
- *The Most Happy Fella*
- *West Side Story*

TARA FASOLINO PECORARO:

- *Annie*
- *A Bronx Tale*
- *Fiddler On the Roof*
- *Grease*
- *Hello, Dolly!*
- *Les Miserables*
- *The Phantom of the Opera*
- *West Side Story*
- *Wicked*

GARY TIFELD:

- *Baby*
- *A Chorus Line*
- *Funny Girl*
- *Gypsy*
- *Hairspray*
- *Les Miserables*
- *My Fair Lady*
- *Ragtime*
- *1776*
- *Sweeney Todd*

ANNETTE TAGLIAFERRO DAIELL:

- *Avenue Q*
- *Company*
- *Funny Girl*
- *Guys and Dolls*
- *Gypsy*
- *Hair*
- *The King and I*
- *The Sound of Music*
- *South Pacific*
- *West Side Story*

JOHN O'HARE:

- *Avenue Q*
- *Chicago*
- *A Day in Hollywood, A Night in the Ukraine*
- *A Funny Thing Happened On the Way to the Forum*
- *Kiss Me, Kate*
- *The Producers*
- *1776*
- *Something Rotten*
- *Spamalot*
- *Urinetown*

JEFFREY TIERNEY:

- *Bonnie and Clyde*
- *The Bridges of Madison County*
- *Cabaret*
- *Heathers*
- *I Love You Because*
- *Memphis*
- *Next to Normal*
- *Passing Strange*
- *Sunday in the Park with George*
- *Urinetown*

How does all of this break down? Let's have a look.

A total of 25 individuals, including myself, submitted lists of their Top-Ten musicals. The shows receiving at least five votes, or 20 percent of the total possible, were, in descending order:

West Side Story - 13

Fiddler On the Roof - 9

Guys and Dolls - 9

The King and I - 9

Gypsy - 8

The Music Man - 8

A Funny Thing Happened On the Way to the Forum - 7

Les Miserables - 6

Sweeney Todd - 6

Carousel - 5

My Fair Lady - 5

Ragtime - 5

South Pacific - 5

Of these, four are **Stephen Sondheim** shows (either as lyricist or as composer/lyricist); three are from the **Rodgers & Hammerstein** canon; nine won Tonys as Best Musical; all have had at least one Broadway revival; and all have been made into motion pictures except *Ragtime*, which is the newest show on the list, having premiered on Broadway on January 18, 1998.

Chapter Eleven

TWO ON THE AISLE

The first Broadway show I saw was *Hello, Dolly!* starring **Ethel Merman**. My ticket cost $2.50. Yes, two dollars and 50 cents. That was July 25, 1970, and, yes, it was a balcony seat. BUT . . . nowadays, shows are charging (and getting) $800 and more, including the recent revival of *Dolly*. To an old-timer like me, that's outrageous!

These thoughts, naturally, led to one of the weekly questions: "What's your take on current ticket prices?" Response was tremendous.

As I put it, "I love theater as much as anyone, but I don't think any show is worth that kind of money. I understand the high costs involved, but I think greed is a large part of this. Theater is meant to be seen by the masses, not just the rich. Wish something could be done to rectify this situation."

My first Broadway show, July 25, 1970.

One friend, **Randy Zeitlin**, with whose wife, **Naomi Zeitlin**, I frequently performed, said simply, "Welcome to the new world."

"I miss the old one sometimes," I responded, offering an opinion I would be willing to bet is shared by many people in my age category.

Ira Rappaport, fellow Queens College-ite and theater devotee: "I was able to see around 50 shows at about that time when I was still at Performing Arts and then off to NYU."

Kathleen Hassett Hochberg, whom I met a couple of years ago when our paths crossed on the Manhattan cabaret scene: "Sad how many shows we have to pass up so that the mortgage can be paid."

Joe Dowd, a fellow journalist whom I had the pleasure of directing in several shows with the Patio Players, including *Fiorello!* and *A Funny Thing Happened On the Way to the Forum*: "I've thought long and hard on your question, Mark, and I don't have an answer. I have long envisioned a theater for classic American musicals, modeled after the Metropolitan Opera, which is heavily subsidized and could do seasons of musicals and, perhaps, classic straight plays. My understanding is the idea has been floated and there are no takers."

Michele Gerrig Newmark: "In Boston [where many Broadway-bound productions did their out-of-town tryouts, a tradition very rarely practiced anymore], if you sat in the rafters and went to a matinee, you paid less than $2.00 in the late '50s-early '60s. We'd rarely go if not for TDF; we usually don't, therefore, see splashy musicals until the ends of their runs."

[TDF, or Theatre Development Fund, is a not-for-profit organization dedicated to making the performing arts financially accessible to everyone. TDF offers discounts up to 70% for members. Annual fee is $40 for those who qualify. In addition, TDF operates several TKTS—short for tickets—booths in New York City, including one in Times Square, the heart of the theater district. The booths offer same-day theater tickets to Broadway and off-Broadway shows at up to 50% off regular prices. Visit tdf.org for further information. In addition, there are many other options available for discounted tickets, if you're willing to do a little online research.]

Alice Goldman Kasten: "It's crazy—and elitist. Theater should be reachable for all. I just saw *Carousel* via TDF from the sixth row of the orchestra for $49. I will say that it scared me, because it made me think it is slated to close—but certainly paying over $100 for a ticket is something most people cannot do. And of course it's not just the ticket—there is transportation, possibly a meal, possibly a baby sitter. Good live theater shouldn't be something you can only see on a very special occasion."

To this, Alice added, "I saw *Hamilton* near the beginning of its run for 'normal' Broadway prices (I think I paid about $125 per ticket) and then, when they realized what they had, they raised the prices to ridiculousness."

Bill Logan, a much-in-demand director on the local theater scene: "My first Broadway show was the original *Company,* 1971, Saturday matinee. Fifth row center orchestra. $8.80. Can't afford Broadway anymore."

Larry Bloom, a dear friend whom I met around 30 years ago on a production of *The Pajama Game,* and with whom I share more theatrical history than just about anyone else: "I agree that ticket prices for Broadway shows are way out of line. Producers are money hungry."

Emily Joyce: "Yes, there are high production costs associated, but also a basic law of economics and pricing is that something is only worth the most that someone will pay for it. As long as people keep paying the exorbitant ticket prices, they'll keep being high."

Barbara Auriemma, another busy director in our neck of the woods with whom I've never worked but whose shows I have seen (and reviewed) quite frequently: "As ridiculous as it may seem, people are paying these exorbitant prices without batting an eye. The only solution is not to support these Broadway shows. There might be an eye-opener if no one is in the audience. Support local theater!"

Stacy Bernstein, a former colleague at Robert F. Kennedy Community High School, a public school in Queens, where we both taught for years: "I have been trying the lottery for *Hamilton* for two years since my daughter decided she wants to see it. Me and everyone else, right? I did get $99 tickets to *Wicked* next week, which is the most I'll pay."

Richard Grillo, a long-time associate from community theater: "It's outrageous!! I just saw *Once On This Island* and got the tickets at TKTS for $125, which was 30% discount!"

JK Larkin: "While theater is meant to be seen by the masses, there is no denying that it is a luxury. Due to the high costs of production of many Broadway shows, few companies can afford to be selling average tickets at anything less than 60 dollars. While it's hard to digest, it's realistic when you evaluate the math backing it up. On the other hand, I have seen upwards of 80 Broadway shows in the last five years, all on my own dollar, and rarely have spent more than 40 dollars on a ticket. It's not difficult to find cheap tickets when one actively seeks them out."

Bridget Phelan-Pezzulich, whom I met online when she responded to my plea for help in setting up a PayPal account so I could try to sell part of my Playbill collection: "My kids see shows pretty often and have never paid that type of money. There are ways of doing it, but they take time and it's not always convenient. There are also apps like TodayTix that offer great prices and many shows are even doing their own lotteries. One thing my kids have done is ask for TodayTix gift cards for birthdays or holidays. Putting a few together gets you a great seat. One other thing they do is try to see the shows in previews or before many reviews come out. If the show gets rave reviews, prices go up. They're savvy theater lovers."

Erik Neilssen, who is involved in just about every aspect of our local theater scene: "As a producer on the community theater circuit, I can speak directly to how staggering the costs of theatrical productions can be. I don't think people realize how much cost is built into doing a show. Just on the community level, our costs keep going up; most groups are doing all they can to keep tickets around $20 a ticket to stay competitive with movie theaters. That's on the community level, when a lot of the people who usually get paid don't get paid, and we beg, borrow and steal whatever we can to put the production together, and we negotiate prices as low as we can wherever we can. Now, take that and multiply it by 1,000,000, when you have to pay union rate to EVERYONE, and high resource costs, and so on and so forth. Then think about all of the productions that crash and burn, that cost way more money than they ever have a prayer of making. It's the law of business that you don't charge people what something costs, you charge what people are willing to pay for it. At the end of the day, the hits help pay for the busts. Producers are in business to make money; if they weren't we wouldn't have shows on the professional level. I wish more people understood and respected the hard work and resources that are needed to make these shows happen. Professionals are putting great value into the productions. I haven't reached the point where it's not worth my time or money . . . yet.

Nothing is easier than TodayTix. It's so easy and affordable. If you haven't used it, check it out."

Melanie Lee: "Broadway prices today are horrifying. It's not right to deprive average-income people, not to mention the poor, of the uplifting, edifying pleasure of seeing a professional live show."

Jack Carr, whom I met on line, as I recall, via a discussion on the merits of composer **Frank Wildhorn's** musicals: "I ushered for the first time recently at the world-famous Glimmerglass (opera) Festival in Cooperstown, New York. One theatergoer in one of the fancier sections dropped her matinee ticket: $131. Then I realized that I was one of the younger people in the house. If theater and opera cater only to the wealthy among us, and the elderly among us, what happens to the future?"

Sharon Weinman, a good friend with whom I once shared the stage in a musical revue, and who is one of the funniest people I know: "Okay, Mark . . . MY two cents . . . In some countries theater is subsidized. It says a lot about a society on how much it values the arts and sees it as a tool for education, self-expression and illuminating the human condition. When I was in high school and college, I would see shows every weekend. I would get standing room tickets. Many theaters used volunteer ushers. The best bet is off-Broadway, because it is more intimate, less expensive and great quality. Lately, I have just been going to Broadway shows on special occasions."

Chapter Twelve

SECOND-ACTING: A THROWBACK TO DAYS GONE BY

S econd-acting a show is a practice that I don't think is, well, practiced, nearly as frequently as it once was. It refers to the, well, act, of non-ticket holders—usually young people who can't afford tickets—waiting outside a theater until intermission (and we used to know when every show would break!) and then making their way into the theater with the intermission crowd and catching the second act of a show.

As we entered, we would pick up a Playbill from the stacks that were generally for the taking at the top of each aisle. (Since selling Playbills on eBay has become so lucrative, they're sometimes harder to come by at the theater these days.) We'd wait for the houselights to dim and then find a couple of empty seats and make a beeline in their direction, just as the second act curtain was about to rise. More often than not, we didn't get to sit together, but beggars can't be choosers.

My friends and I used to second-act back in the days when we were still in college (mid-1970s, for the most part). We didn't do it often, but enough times to have accumulated a few interesting stories. I should point out that security back then wasn't nearly as tight at the theaters (or anywhere, for that matter) as it became post 9/11. You didn't have to show your ticket for re-admission to the theater. And it seems to me that many more people used to emerge from the theater back then at intermission, with most of them taking advantage of the opportunity to grab a cigarette. So, it was very easy to get lost in the crowd.

I must have second-acted four or five shows altogether—all musicals. Seeing half a straight play did not appeal to me. I remember seeing the second half of *A Little Night Music*, after having seen the entire show already. I loved it so much more during the second go-round. And I got to see act two of *Jerry's Girls*, which was, of course, a revue based on **Jerry Herman**'s songbook, so there was no plot to worry about.

But I most memorably second-acted *Lorelei*, starring **Carol Channing**, at the Palace Theatre. On that particular day, as I described it on my Facebook page, a couple left the theater, apparently not planning to return. My friend and I asked if we could have their ticket stubs, which they gave us. We now entered the theater with "our" tickets, took "our" seats and found ourselves being harassed by the couple next to us. They were friends of the couple that left and told us those were not our seats. They called over an usher to complain. The usher asked if we had our tickets, which we promptly produced. End of story!

I've thought about this incident many times over the years. Our "neighbors" could have been nice about it all, politely asking how we happened to get their friends' tickets. (I assume their friends had told them they were leaving.) We would have happily explained. But they were so unnecessarily nasty about it that we decided not to let on. They must have thought we had mugged their friends outside the theater and stolen their stubs. I'd be willing to bet the incident preoccupied them for the rest of the show. Well, at least I hope it did!

So, how did some of my friends respond to my question about this all-but-forgotten phenomenon?

Evan Ross, a true man of the theater who used to direct some of the productions at my alma mater, Queens College: "Spent most of my high school years second-acting everything from *Side By Side By Sondheim* to *They're Playing Our Song . . .* "

Marilyn Garfinkel: "I've not done this, but my older sister, Gail, saw the second act of *The Front Page* numerous times during the 1969/1970 revival. She was clearly a big fan. And back then no one questioned it or even seemed to care."

Gary Tifeld: "I don't know if this counts as 'second-acting,' but you tell me. In 1981, my father was taking his girlfriend and her younger son to see *Annie,* which they had never seen. I'd already seen it twice, but I had tickets to see another show that same night. The plan was that I would come meet them outside their theater after my show was over so we could go home together. My show ended up being shorter than I realized and I was out of that theater by about 9:45. So I walked over to the theater where *Annie* was running (the August Wilson, the ANTA at the time) where the second act had just gotten underway. If you know that theater, you know that when you enter, you go down a few steps into the lobby, which is like a big lounge with several couches and chairs. There is a stairway there which leads up to the rear of the orchestra. I took a seat and started reading my

Playbill. There was an usherette also in the lobby hanging out with another theater employee and she asked if she could help me. I explained and was it all right for me to sit there and wait? She said, 'Sure, no problem,' and I went back to reading. I could hear the show from upstairs and could tell it was the start of the FDR scene, before the 'Tomorrow' reprise. Less than a minute later, the usherette asked me if I'd like to just go upstairs and watch the rest of the show. It had already been running a few years now so it wasn't SRO anymore and there were several empty rows at the back. So I did. Now when people ask me how many times I saw *Annie* on Broadway, I say, "Two and a third.'"

I'd call that "unintentional second-acting!"

A couple of people, interestingly, adapted the custom to suit their own particular pleasures.

Guy DeMatties, who covered me in a production of *Charlotte's Web* with Plaza Productions (as I will discuss a bit later in chapter 14), surprised me when he wrote: "Geez, I never thought of doing that. It never occurred to me to try to see the second half of a show. I HAVE done it at the ballpark and seen second halves of games, but never a show."

Larry Bloom: "I never did this! Too much love for theater, I guess! I have done this in the movies!"

I replied to Larry, "We did it BECAUSE we loved the theater. If we didn't, why would we have bothered? Funny, but I never did this at the movies."

Larry conceded: "You're right!"

Joe Schuchman, one of my best friends during our college days together (and a subsequent *Phoenix* Arts Editor) and whom I see far too little of these days, then asked, "How would you even go about second-acting a movie?"

To this, I responded, "I guess he meant walking in in the middle. In the old days, there were many theaters that showed films continuously, so I guess you could have always caught up."

Bill Logan turned the tables on us: "Never second-act-ed, but I did walk out on one show at the intermission. Just once."

That's what I'd call a reverse second-act-er!

Similarly, **Michele Gerrig Newmark** explained: "Never did it, but we've given ballet tickets to people outside the theater when we've left before the end of a performance."

Debbie Vogel: "I used to want to see the whole show, so I'd buy standing room tickets. There's always someone who for whatever reason leaves at intermission, so usually I was able to find a seat for the second act."

Gary Tifeld: "Yeah, I've definitely done that. Each time I've gone SRO to a show, I've always found an empty seat to move into. On one occasion, I got a seat at TKTS for a balcony seat, then went downstairs and stood in the back of the orchestra instead."

Debbie Vogel: "You have a better view standing than all the way in the back of the balcony."

Neil Einleger, whom I've come to know on Facebook through our shared theatrical interests, said, "It is, sadly, completely verboten in this day and age. It is considered 'theft of services.' If you go outside the lobby area at intermission, say for a smoke or phone call, you must show your ticket for re-admittance."

Debbie Vogel corroborated: "People used to be able to enter the theater after intermission and no one checked tickets. Now, if you leave the theater, your ticket is scanned out and then when you return you're scanned back in. We have heightened security. Now also packages are checked by security."

Times sure have changed!

Chapter Thirteen

DINNER WITH MARLO THOMAS . . . SORT OF

The Facebook posting that ultimately led to the idea for this book gave the responders to my weekly theater question the opportunity to ask me questions, which I thoroughly enjoyed answering. I even expect to use some of those questions in future weeks to see how my friends would answer them. With all this in mind, I asked the following question: "If you could interview one theatrical luminary and ask him/her one question, who and what?"

By now you know of my admiration of **Harold Prince**, so it was probably no surprise to anyone that I responded, "I would like to ask producer/director **Harold Prince** how he views his place in theatrical history. I, for one, think he is in a category all his own."

My friends came up with some very interesting choices and some equally insightful questions they would like to pose.

Marilyn Garfinkel: "I would like to interview **Mel Brooks** and ask him how he's kept his creativity alive for so many years. I'd also like to ask him the favorite actors that he's worked with and what production he's most proud of."

Jacqueline Schnapp Schwartz: "I would interview **Leonard Bernstein** and ask him how he would encourage young people to appreciate the arts."

Neil Einleger: "I would probably go with **Oscar Hammerstein II** because he began the concept musical and recreated its form several times. My question would be, 'What do you look for in the text to elaborate into song?'"

Lloyd Baum: "I would ask **George Gershwin** which gave him more pleasure, his popular songs or his orchestral pieces."

Richard Bergman, father of a former student of mine with whom I've kept in touch: "I would like to ask **Hugh Jackman** if he enjoyed playing **Peter Allen** as much as he appeared to be and, disregarding the money effect, would he rather do theater or film?"

Mitchell Kessler: "As an amateur, I can understand how one can maintain enthusiasm for a few performances as the climax after months of rehearsals. I would ask any Broadway actor who has fulfilled a one-year contract, 'How do you keep your performances at fever pitch and at such a high caliber day after day, week after week, so seven months in, a Thursday night audience gets the same performance the opening night audience got?'"

Michael Brooks: "I would ask **Barbra Streisand**, 'Which character did you enjoy portraying the most?'"

Bruce Bider: "I would ask **Al Jolson**, 'How would you explain the employment of blackface to a society conditioned to reject it, and how do you think your career might have been different had you not used it?'" To this, Bider went on to add, "Even though I object to the blackface from a modern perspective, I love Jolson as a singer and all-around entertainer."

Michele Gerrig Newmark: "I would have a double interview with **Liza Minnelli** and **Carrie Fisher**: How were you able to emerge from under the cloaks of famous parents and find your own voices?"

Over the years, as a reporter for both my college newspaper and as a professional journalist, I have had quite a few opportunities to interview celebrities, mostly in the entertainment field. The most memorable experience I had along these lines involved **Marlo Thomas**, perhaps still best remembered for her popular television series, *That Girl*, despite an extensive career that has encompassed motion pictures and a considerable amount of stage work, in addition to many other notable small-screen appearances. Of course, today she is the face of St. Jude Children's Research Hospital in Memphis, Tennessee, which was founded by her father, entertainer **Danny Thomas**.

My encounter with Miss Thomas happened while I was writing for *Phoenix* at Queens College. It is an experience I have never forgotten, one which I have recounted countless times.

Miss Thomas was starring on Broadway at the time, in a comedy called *Thieves*, written by her then-boyfriend, **Herb Gardner**. Through a twist of fate, it marked Miss Thomas's debut on the Great White Way. The play was out of town prior to arriving in New York when it became apparent that the leading lady was decidedly wrong for the role of Sally, a strong-willed New

Yorker who was long on the verge of divorce. When no one else turned up to replace her predecessor, Miss Thomas's own fighting instincts led her to take on the responsibility, knowing the play's very life depended on her. The play, which featured a cast that included **Richard Mulligan**, **Dick Van Patten**, **Ann Wedgeworth**, **Irwin Corey** and **David Spielberg**, all under the direction of **Charles Grodin**, ended up having a healthy nine-month run.

As Arts Editor of the newspaper, I established a column called "Getting To Know . . . ," which featured periodic in-depth interviews with people in the entertainment field. [Notice how I sneaked a *King and I* reference in there?] I managed to arrange an interview with Miss Thomas, which was supposed to take place at the theater following an evening performance of the play.

Getting To Know . . .

MARLO THOMAS

Our interview with Marlo Thomas in the Queens College Phoenix newspaper, including the chauffer-delivered photograph. Note the King and I reference in the column's title.

I attended the show with **Brenda Shactman**, a dear friend and colleague from the newspaper who would assist with the interview.

Knowing I was to meet Miss Thomas, I was unable to concentrate on the play itself, so I remember very little of it . . . reminiscent of my experience seeing *The King and I* at Damrosch Park, which, similarly, remains a blur.

After the show, Brenda and I made our way to the stage door of the Broadhurst Theatre, expecting to be greeted by the proverbial doorman and escorted to Miss Thomas's dressing room for the interview. But no one seemed to be around. So we decided just to wait . . . and wait . . . and wait . . .

Could they have forgotten our appointment? Many minutes went by and still nobody. Then, the lights began to go dark. Brenda and I looked at each other in disbelief. How could they have done this to us, we wondered?

We were about to leave, feeling totally dejected, when a door opened and there stood Miss Thomas herself.

"Hello, I'm Marlo," she said, as if an introduction was necessary. She was wearing her fur coat, carrying some belongings, and looked ready to head out into the chilly, rainy night. We introduced ourselves and secretly guessed—quite correctly—that our dressing room interview was not to be.

But something even better was in store.

We followed Miss Thomas—by now we had been invited to call her Marlo—out of the building to a waiting limousine. The chauffeur opened the doors for us (I, in my innocence, nearly sat in the front next to the driver's seat, realizing just in the nick of time that we were all expected to sit together in the back), and we drove off into the night. We rode around for what seemed like a good 45 minutes, finally arriving at our destination: a restaurant that—years later—I realized was literally around the corner from the theater. It was the heavy New York after-theater traffic that had delayed our arrival.

As we pulled up at the restaurant, the wait staff greeted our celebrity friend by name: "Good evening, Miss Thomas. How are you tonight, Miss Thomas?" all the while holding up umbrellas as they escorted her from the car. Brenda and I fended for ourselves!

We were seated and Marlo began to peruse the menu. We did, too . . . and, as a couple of college kids, with a total of maybe

$1.50 in our pockets between us, felt a sudden panic. At best, we could afford to split a glass of water!

As an appetizer, Marlo ordered a shrimp cocktail, with baby lamb chops as her entree. As I recall, the two dishes came to a total of about $50, a very hefty tab back in the '70s! Marlo turned to us and asked what we'd like to have.

"You know," I said, thinking as quickly as I could, "we had a big dinner just before the show and we're still stuffed." I think we ended up ordering a soda.

"Are you sure you don't want to eat anything?" Marlo kept asking.

"Oh, no, we're good," I said, asking if we might begin the interview while waiting for the meal to arrive.

I turned on my little reel-to-reel tape recorder, the latest in technology at the time. We both felt at ease with Marlo from the outset, and we began to chat—much as old friends might do.

Brenda unconsciously began to rub her arms with her hands, an effort to warm herself up in the air-conditioned room.

Marlo took note and, without missing a beat, called over a waiter.

"Would you have an extra jacket that my friend can borrow? She's freezing," she said.

He did not; each waiter had only his own jacket, and was not allowed to remove it while on duty.

"Could you bring us a tablecloth?" Marlo asked.

The waiter brought one and gave it to Marlo, who passed it on to Brenda, suggesting she wrap herself in it.

Brenda was understandably embarrassed by all the attention, but the cold got the best of her. Draping it over her shoulders, she said, "I can't believe I'm having dinner with **Marlo Thomas** wrapped in a tablecloth!"

We managed to get in a few questions before dinner arrived. In truth, Brenda and I were starving and the food looked amazing, but we managed to keep our hunger under wraps and continued to chat with Marlo, off the record, while she ate.

I asked if she would be able to provide a photo of herself to run with the story. [Again, this was long before selfies!] She said she would have her driver drop it off in the newspaper room the next day.

When the time came to leave, Marlo offered to have her driver take us home.

"We live in Queens," Brenda said, which was a bit further than Marlo had anticipated.

"Can I have the driver drop you off at the subway, then?" she asked.

As I recall, we declined the offer. We were about to part ways, when Marlo, noting the inclement weather, turned to Brenda and said, "Why don't you borrow my fur coat? My driver can pick it up when he delivers the picture tomorrow."

"Umm, we're going on the subway," Brenda said pointedly. "I don't think I should be wearing a fur coat on the subway." She thanked Marlo for being so considerate and we all headed home.

Sure enough, bright and early the next morning, the chauffeur delivered a photo of Marlo, along with a note from her:

> "Dear Mark—It was terrific meeting you both. I can't wait to read your article. Love, Marlo."

The story—and the photo—ran a few days later. I sent Marlo a copy of the article, which ended with the line, "Meeting her was a most rewarding experience."

To my amazement, not long after, I received a letter in the mail from Marlo:

> "Dear Mark & Brenda, What can I say? Your article on me was just terrific. I'm glad you liked me as much as I liked you. But, even more to the point—is your talents. It was one of the few articles ever written on me that didn't misquote or misunderstand what I was trying to say. I especially thank you for that. Good luck with your new term. And thanks, too, for a rewarding experience. Love, Marlo."

Marlo Thomas' letter commenting on the article that we wrote about her in the Queens College Phoenix newspaper

Chapter Fourteen

MUST THE SHOW GO ON?

The passing of **Carol Channing**, known to almost never miss a performance, got me wondering: What do people think of Broadway performers who don't seem to share the old belief that "the show must go on"?

This was a question I posed one Friday morning on my Facebook page, leading to one of the more "lively" discussions.

As I suggested at the time, "I know there are some people who believe actors, like everyone else, are entitled to take days off. However, it seems that many of today's leading players miss performances for some rather trivial reasons. It is the dream of most actors to make it to Broadway. Once they are there, I think it comes with extra responsibility to show up if at all possible. I remember on one ticket-buying binge several years ago, going from theater to theater, I noticed that SIX star performers were all out of their respective shows that day. Can't imagine what Ms. Channing would have thought of that."

Joan Barber, a Broadway veteran who recently starred in a show I stage managed, had this to say: "I believe the show must go on, not I must go on. I've actually been sent home by a stage manager when my coughing scared him so much he thought I'd infect the entire cast. I learned my lesson. I'm not that important."

My response to Joan, who impresses me as one who takes her work very seriously, was as follows: "An interesting perspective. You may not have gone on, but you were there, ready to do your job. It was probably best that you didn't, but it wasn't for lack of trying. I sometimes get the feeling that today's 'stars' don't appreciate the position they're in as much as they should. Maybe I'm wrong . . . who knows?"

Well, as it turned out, most of my friends seemed to agree with me . . . that missing performances, especially on Broadway, is not an easily forgivable transgression. Many pointed to partic- ular performers to make their points.

Larry Bloom: "**Merman** never missed a performance. A good example to emulate."

Bill Logan: "I saw **Sammy Davis, Jr.** in *Golden Boy* when he went on with laryngitis. He still sounded better than most singers."

Mitchell Kessler: "For the leads, if they are a name or their performance drove people to the theater or if they are highly paid, only illness or death in the family excuses them. I saw **Bernadette Peters** in *The Goodbye Girl* when she had a cold. Kudos to her."

"The night I saw it," I responded, "she had a cold. I wonder if we saw it around the same time . . . or did she have a cold frequently? All I remember was **Martin Short** was wonderful and Bernadette was blah."

Bruce Bider: "When I saw it, she did not have a cold and was wonderful, too."

Tracey Berse Simon: "This is bringing back memories. When **Danny Kaye** was in *Two By Two*, he had broken his leg. We worried that he was going to drop out, but he didn't. He played Noah from a wheelchair (willing suspension of disbelief) and on crutches. He even stayed on stage after the show to talk to the audience."

Michele Gerrig Newmark: "**Audra McDonald** has been out almost every time we've gone to see one of her starring vehicles. Her understudy in *Carousel* was great. Her Bess replacement was merely adequate. I didn't pay to see an adequate performance. I am NOT the president of Audra's fan club."

Alison Feuer Pascuzzi: "I enjoyed her dancing and singing in *Shuffle Along*. She didn't call in even though she was six months pregnant and age 46."

Bill Logan: "I hear she doesn't miss very much anymore, since right after *Marie Christine* the doctors found that she had a tendency for extremely low blood sugar which was causing all her problems."

Michele Gerrig Newmark: "I saw her in *Ragtime* and *110 in the Shade*. She is SO gifted, which is why it was SO disappointing when she was not performing."

Bill Logan: "During the original run of *Hairspray*, **Harvey Fierstein** famously blasted the younger members of the cast for this very issue."

Tracey Berse Simon: "I took my mom to see *Hairspray* for Mother's Day. **Bruce Villanch** [one of Fierstein's future replacements] and, if I recall correctly, **Dick Latessa**, were the only featured cast members to show up. However, it being a young cast, I can imagine they'd want to be with their moms."

I was not supportive of this response. "How did you feel about that—having most of the cast out?" I asked. "Do you really think Mother's Day is a valid reason for missing a show on Broadway? A position people would kill to be in? Couldn't they see their mothers later in the day, maybe? I'm sure there were plenty of other talented actors around who would love to have had the opportunity to be in their shoes."

Tracey Berse Simon: "But there are others who will say, 'There will be more shows, but you only have one mother!' Jewish guilt there!"

I was not suggesting they needed to pick one or the other. "Surely there was a way to perform in a show and see their mothers, too," I wrote, adding, "By the way, I also don't get those who think their birthday is a reason to not go to school or to work. Sure, celebrate. But live up to your responsibilities, too."

As for **Bill Logan**'s comment about **Harvey Fierstein**, I said, "He's from the old school. I'd bet there are leads on Broadway today who have missed more performances during the run of one show than **Merman, Martin, Channing**, well, you name 'em, missed in their entire combined careers."

Tracey Berse Simon: "When we went to see *Forum*, **Nathan Lane** decided not to appear that night. I think they said he was saving his voice to sing the national anthem at Yankee Stadium or he had just done that the day before. We had bought the tickets just to see him. We could've turned them in for another date in the near future (**Whoopi Goldberg** was starting in a week), but we had other plans. If they had let us swap them for tickets a few weeks later, we could have. However, the understudy was great, as was the rest of the cast."

My response? "I find that so disrespectful of the audience. He surely knows people specifically want to see him."

Neil Einleger: "When **Kaye Ballard** went into *Pirates of Penzance* as Ruth, she was shocked at how little it took for actors to call out . . . 'sprained ankle? . . . in my day, the entire foot would need to be missing!!!'"

Emily Joyce: "I have a friend who played Cassie in my high school's production of *A Chorus Line*. She did closing night on a sprained ankle and was on crutches for the rest of the school year. Now, imagine doing a Broadway production of *A Chorus Line* on a sprained ankle, and not just one night, further injuring yourself, and putting yourself in a position to not be able to work for weeks, months, or even years, plus reparative surgeries and physical therapy that's needed after exacerbating an injury that could have healed by itself with a week of bed rest."

Neil Einleger: "As someone who has worked on Broadway, I will tell you that, for sure, the work ethic is NOT THE SAME AS IT USED TO BE!"

Emily Joyce: "Yes, but demands are also higher, and pay has not kept up with the cost of living and everyone in this country is jaded. Some decline in work ethic is expected and justified. Maybe it's decreased below what's expected, but it's harder now than it was. As a young theater professional on the daily grind, it's hard out there."

Debbie Vogel: "Yes, doing eight shows a week is grueling, but Broadway show contract minimums are far over the cost of living."

Michael Wolf, an old acquaintance from my Queens College days, with whom I once performed in a local production of *Mame:* "Ms. Joyce makes many valid points. But Mr. Einleger does as well."

[Reminds me of that line in *Fiddler* . . . I suspect many of you who are reading this will get the reference, so no need to go further on that! LOL]

Others weighed in with various comments related to the discussion.

Erik Neilssen: "I don't do theater professionally, but if I did, I doubt I would miss a day of it! Mostly because I love it. I don't miss work now unless I'm hospitalized. I doubt that would change, if I were getting paid to do the thing I love most."

Marilyn Garfinkel: "With the cost of seeing a Broadway show going through the roof, I think the cast, especially the leads, should do their very best to be there. Unless there is something seriously wrong with the actor, of course. It is so disappointing to pay big bucks, look forward to a show, and hear the dreaded announcement, 'In today's performance, _____ will be playing the role of _____.'"

Emily Joyce: "I seem to be the only one with this perspective but I think we are beginning to demand too much from Broadway actors. Expectations at the stage door, press appearances, media, public engagements, public service announcements, etc . . . on top of the task of eight performances a week, all with varying degrees of emotional, physical, and mental demands of one's body. The average American 'full-time' position is 40 hours/week, with reasonable time off each week (usually two days the way it works out) and regular, steady pay. Actors work six days a week, with two of those days being two-a-days, amounting to between 5-10 hours/day just in performance, not to mention rehearsals, tech, pickups, and all the aforementioned media and engagement expectations. There's no reason to be upset with the actors that they didn't give you your money's worth when they have no say in the pricing of tickets, usually. I go to Broadway for the experience and the appreciation for the art form, not specifically to see a name. Actors are people, too, and shouldn't be held to some unattainable and unrealistic standard."

To Emily, I replied, "I think a lot has always been expected of Broadway stars. I don't think they're expected to do any more today than previously. I've been a Broadway fan for 50 years and have always waited at stage doors for actors to come out. Many of them did and were generally gracious. And actors have always had to promote their shows. I think the phenomenon of calling in is just a reflection of our times. People, in general, no longer show the same dedication and responsibility that they used to . . . in pretty much every facet of life. I guess actors are like everyone else in that sense. I, for one, have always admired actors' show-must-go-on attitude. That seems more and more a thing of the past."

Bridget Phelan-Pezzulich: "Social media takeovers are another newly added demand. Having to do hour-long live streams of backstage 'exclusives' gives less time for vocal rest. Actors . . .

now must have a social media session, or behind-the-scenes bonus sessions with fans from all over the world via the Internet. It does take a toll."

I agreed that "there are a lot of demands, yes. But there have always been, I think, just of a different sort. They used to do the talk show circuit, which hardly exists anymore. They always had to do interviews and other forms of publicity. I can liken this discussion to teaching careers. I took pride in missing very few days of work. I had colleagues who believed in using up their 10 sick days every year even if they were never sick. They would take days off on their birthdays, because they were tired, because of snow, because of heat, because of . . . well, you get the idea. Teaching is rather comparable to performing, I think. We teach five classes a day, adding up to about 3 1/2 hours in front of the classroom. That's an awful lot of talking. And it's exhausting. So, I credit all those teachers who made it through each day without taking time off. And as for those who took off at the drop of a hat, I always thought it was less than professional, leaving the rest of us to pick up an extra class to cover theirs. I think similarly of the Broadway situation. Maybe I'm old-fashioned, but to me commitment means something. I think this is something lacking in some of the younger people nowadays."

Gary Eisele: "To this day, people still comment about how I played piano, in church, during my father's funeral. And then I played a show performance less than two hours after the funeral ended. Above and beyond—no, I don't think so."

On a related issue, **Joseph Schweigert,** who I've directed and appeared with on local stages, asked: "If anybody knows, how much notice do understudies have before they go on?"

Debbie Vogel: "Sometimes just minutes. I witnessed a performance where the lead tried to make it in, but because of horrific weather, couldn't get to the theater. The understudy did a fabulous job. Also, actors have gotten sick in the middle of a performance and the understudy (who is normally in the ensemble) takes over the role mid-show (a swing takes over the ensemble track). Those are extreme emergencies. An actor is supposed to give at least 1/2 hour notice if he's calling out. For the lead's vacation, the understudy knows weeks in advance."

As an addendum to this discussion, several days later I wrote on Facebook: "Related to this week's theater question: Just came from seeing a Broadway show that opened about six weeks ago. We were supposed to go last month, but the leading lady was out, so we decided to go today instead. Guess what? She was out again. I asked an usher (a young lady) if she's ever in the show. With a straight face, she said, 'Yes. She's only been out four times this month.' It seems the honor of being on Broadway ain't what it used to be. I rest my case about the lack of strong work ethics nowadays."

Addendum number two: I mentioned earlier about meeting **Guy DeMatties** when he covered me in *Charlotte's Web* in a touring production on Long Island. At that point, I had been performing for somewhere around 30 years and always prided myself on never having missed a performance. Well, the flu season got the better of me that year—boy, did it ever. I literally didn't have the strength to get out of bed and I ended up missing an entire week of performances—amounting to four or five, I believe it was. Luckily, Guy and I had both been cast to alternate in the role during the extended tour, so he was more than ready to go on. Even more luckily, he was available when we needed him!

Chapter Fifteen

IF YOU COULD GO BACK IN TIME...

I always used to get jealous when people would reminisce about having attended a big opening night on Broadway or talk about how they had seen a particular show in its original run.

"I saw *My Fair Lady* with **Rex Harrison** and **Julie Andrews**," someone might say. And I would be in awe, anticipating all the details of what it must have been like. When it came to most of those classic shows, I could only say that I saw, at best, the first revival. As good as some of them were, it just wasn't the same —it didn't carry the same historical significance.

I did get to see **Yul Brynner** recreate his iconic role in *The King and I* in its 1977 revival, with an incandescent **Constance Towers** opposite him as Anna. But how I ultimately got to see the show was, I think, rather surprising.

Of course, as *The King and I* meant so much to me, I had been wanting to see it very badly, but the tickets were prohibitively expensive, going for the then-exorbitant top price of $16.50. One day, I was with my friend, **Alan Rothkopf**, on line at the TKTS booth in Duffy Square, where tickets are available at discounted prices on the day of a performance. We were open to seeing pretty much any good show that was listed on the board. *The King and I,* alas, was not among the offerings.

As we waited, a man passed by, hawking a pair of tickets to the very show I had been most anxious to see. Naturally, my ears perked up, along with my inbred native New Yorker's suspicions. I stopped him and we began to do business. He was selling the tickets very cheaply, as I recall, almost too cheaply, I thought at the time, though I'm no longer sure of the exact price. Somehow $10 apiece sounds about right. It was too good to be true.

I told him we were interested, but I would need to verify the authenticity of the tickets before handing over the cash. Even in those more innocent days there were people out there looking to make a quick buck at someone else's expense.

"Would you mind walking with me over to the theater so we could check them out?" I asked. I half expected him to spin on his heels and disappear but, to my surprise, he agreed. I left Alan to hold our place in line and the gentleman and I walked over to the Uris Theatre (now the Gershwin), a few blocks uptown.

The box office attendant verified that the tickets were legitimate, the money and the tickets changed hands, and Alan and I were set.

Around that time, I also had the opportunity to attend a record signing at E.J. Korvette on Fifth Avenue when the new cast recording of the show was released. I got to meet both **Yul Brynner** and **Constance Towers,** and they graciously signed my album. Luckily, nothing resembling my embarrassing **Ethel Merman** record-signing fiasco took place. (See chapter 19.)

Meeting "The King" himself, Yul Brynner, and his Anna, Constance Towers. That's press agent Joshua Ellis in the foreground.

By the time Brynner brought the show to Broadway yet again in 1985, he had been diagnosed with inoperable lung cancer, with less than a year to live. It had been reported that at some performances he was too weak to perform his signature song, "A Puzzlement," which was eliminated, and in the "Shall We Dance?" sequence, his latest leading lady, **Mary Beth Peil**, was left to perform it alone, as Brynner watched. As much as I wanted to see him one last time, I refused to go under those conditions. I preferred to keep my memories of his vigorous portrayal of the Siamese monarch intact.

I am also thrilled to have seen **Carol Channing** in the first revival of her career-defining performance in *Hello, Dolly!,* which returned to Broadway in 1978, only eight years after the record-setting run of the original ended. It brought back so many memories of when I had seen it earlier with **Ethel Merman** as Dolly.

As for that other classic, *My Fair Lady*, I greatly enjoyed the revival that starred **Ian Richardson**, **Christine Andreas**, **Robert Coote** (recreating his original role of Colonel Pickering) and **George Rose**, who played Eliza's no-good father, Alfred P. Doolittle, to the hilt. Rose's performance was surprisingly nominated for a Tony Award as Best Leading Actor In a Musical in a role that, 20 years earlier, had earned its creator, **Stanley Holloway**, a nomination in the Supporting or Featured Actor in a Musical category. And Rose ended up winning, besting fellow nominee Richardson, as well as **Mako**, who starred in *Pacific Overtures*, and **Jerry Orbach**, leading man of the original production of *Chicago*.

Speaking of *Chicago*, here was a case where I actually got to see the original production of this now-landmark musical, giving me the opportunity to see not only Orbach but **Gwen Verdon** and **Chita Rivera** at the top of their game. Now, when I tell someone that I actually saw that show, I imagine they feel much as I did when others told me of their early theatergoing days. I guess it's one of the perks of getting older!

Perhaps my greatest bragging rights come courtesy of the original production of *Follies*, which I saw near the tail end of its 15-month run, with the leads and many of the featured performers still firmly in place.

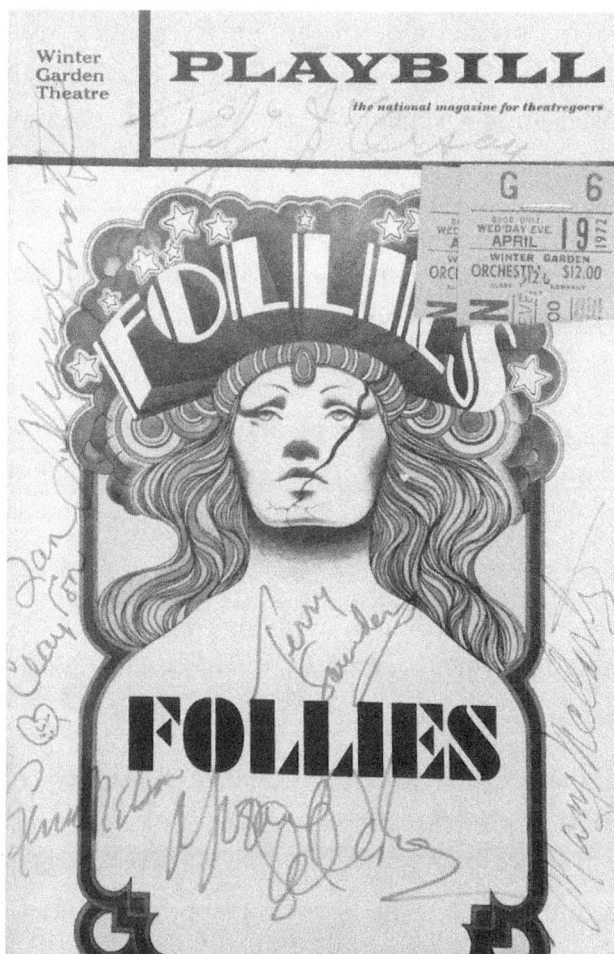

One of my theatrical "bragging rights," seeing the first Broadway production of Follies *and meeting most of the original cast after the show.*

Follies, in fact, was one of the shows I got to review for *Phoenix*. I hadn't seen the review in perhaps 40 years—until it recently crossed my mind.

Of *Follies*, I wrote, in part, "From the start, we know we are in for an elaborate evening in the theatre. **James Goldman**'s libretto is not as interesting as it could have been. The brilliance of **Stephen Sondheim's** music and lyrics is apparent. The marvelous cast is given the opportunity to display its talents." I also praised **Boris Aronson's** "stylish set" and "the simply spectacular costumes" designed by **Florence Klotz**.

It was one of the earliest reviews I wrote. In retrospect, I should have been much more impressed with what I had seen. Today, *Follies* is one of my all-time favorite shows. And I was there near the beginning of its existence.

All of this is brought to mind by another Weekly Theater Question: If you could go back in time to be at the opening night performance of any show in Broadway history, what would it be?

I didn't need long to come up with my own answer: "I'd have to say *Funny Girl*. I can't even imagine what it must have been like to discover a blazing new star like **Ms. Streisand**."

Right off the bat, several of my friends cast their votes for *Show Boat*, a musical play that first opened on Broadway on December 27, 1927. Produced by the great impresario **Florenz Ziegfeld** and featuring music by **Jerome Kern** and a book and lyrics by **Oscar Hammerstein II**, based on the **Edna Ferber** novel of the same name, the show marked a radical departure from the light operettas and musical revues that preceded it, including some of Ziegfeld's own lavish productions.

Here are some of the comments expressed on Facebook.

Mitchell Kessler would have liked to attend opening night because "it changed everything. Ziegfeld did not know how it would go. Also, to see the audience reaction to this new kind of Broadway. Plus the score. Plus **Paul Robeson**."

Bruce Bider, who chose the same landmark event, appropriately corrected one of Kessler's points. "Robeson was in the original London and the first Broadway revival in 1932," he wrote. "The original Broadway Joe was a man named **Jules Bledsoe**." Joe, of course, is a stevedore in the show who sings its most famous song, "Ol' Man River." Over time, the part has become most closely identified with Robeson, for whom the role was originally written but who, because of an unanticipated delay in the show's opening, became unavailable for its New York debut.

Ron Spivak, a professional actor and writer with whom I became friends on Facebook, had the same idea: "Definitely *Show Boat*, for the same reasons as Mitchell. After that, perhaps *The Black Crook*. I'm sure that by today's standards, I'd find it God-awful . . . but fascinating."

In some corners, *The Black Crook* is considered the prototype of the modern musical, though many dispute this claim. The show opened on September 12, 1866. Reports indicate that its running time was a staggering five and a half hours. Still, it managed to run an impressive 474 performances.

In *Complete Book of the American Musical Theater*, its author **David Ewen** suggests that *The Black Crook* was "the most successful musical production of any genre seen in this country" up to that point. "Its significance," he continues, "rests not merely on its box-office appeal but more specifically on the fact that it was the first musical in America to indicate some of the procedures of later stage productions."

The show, which incorporated elements of **Goethe's** *Faust* and was perhaps most notable for its eye-popping special effects and skimpy costumes, was subsequently revived multiple times.

West Side Story, like *Show Boat*, has become a landmark in the musical theater, despite or perhaps because of its surprisingly dark overtones (before the final curtain, three of its leading characters would die), intricate musical score and heavy use of dance to propel its *Romeo and Juliet*-based tale set amidst the rivalry between two teenage street gangs in 1950s New York City. In my informal survey, it received multiple mentions, including one by **Marilyn Garfinkel**, who opined: "It has such great music and dancing . . . as well as an important message."

Another adaptation of a classic British literary work, the musical *My Fair Lady* was also a popular choice.

"Wouldn't it be loverly," **Debbie Vogel** responded, calling to mind one of the show's memorable songs, "to have been at the opening night in 1956? Many people in the theatrical community didn't have faith that *Pygmalion* would make a good musical. **Rodgers & Hammerstein** turned down the opportunity."

Directly addressing the show's creators, she added, "Thank you, **Lerner & Loewe**, for a classic."

As **David Sheward** writes in his book, *It's a Hit*, "Like so many other smash hits, *My Fair Lady* was not given a ghost of a chance by most Broadway professionals when it was first conceived. Many talents, such as **Rodgers & Hammerstein** . . . had essayed musicalizing **Bernard Shaw's** *Pygmalion*." He goes on to explain they turned it down because "the play is a non-love story. They also found it difficult to cut any of Shaw's brilliant dialogue."

The Broadway opening of the original production of *Gypsy* on May 21, 1959, the last show to arrive that season, is another one several acquaintances would love to have witnessed.

Bill Logan, who said he actually attended another highly coveted performance, the very first New York preview of *Follies,* admitted, "While that would be tough to top, I would have loved to have been at the opening night of *Gypsy* with **Merman**."

Similarly, **Larry Bloom** responded: "My choice would have to be the opening of *Gypsy* starring **Ethel Merman**. I sat with my mother on the aisle in the orchestra seats early in the run and she was truly unforgettable. I could only imagine how the opening night would have been."

That comment inspired **Ron Spivak** to share what became one of my favorite tales of show business: "My dear late voice teacher once told me the story that the night he went to see *Gypsy* he had managed to acquire a very hard-to-get single ticket, on the aisle in the last row of the orchestra. He got stuck in traffic and arrived barely in time. The overture had started, and he slipped into his aisle seat in the dark. Then he noticed a little piece of paper stuck in his Playbill. 'Oh, my God,' he thought. 'Which actor is out of the show tonight?' As he was struggling to read the piece of paper in the dark, he suddenly felt a hand on his shoulder. **Ethel Merman**. She whispered in his ear, 'Never fear, darling, mother is here.' And then she stood up and—right on cue—yelled, 'Sing out, Louise.' My teacher never forgot it."

Another show multiple respondents mentioned is *Fiddler on the Roof.*

Dana Jaffe, a long-time fellow community theater performer, recalled that her first Broadway show, at the age of 12, was, in fact, the **Sholom Aleichem**-inspired musical, in which she saw one of **Zero Mostel's** replacements, **Harry Goz**, as the dairyman

Tevye: "We sat in the last row of the balcony. When we arrived in the balcony, a repairman was high up on a ladder fixing something on the ceiling. My father announced loudly, 'There's the fiddler on the roof.' The show was great."

Miles Tepper: "I would have to say *Fiddler on the Roof*. Aside from seeing **Zero** [one of those one-name-is-all-you-need wonders] in the lead, the show itself strikes home, since all my relatives came from there, and my mother was born not far from Anatevka. And, of course, it's incredibly moving (and darkly funny) as well."

Interestingly, there is much skepticism as to whether the town of Anatevka ever existed. It is generally believed that it is a purely fictional place, drawn from the imagination of **Sholom Aleichem**.

To better prepare himself to play the role of Motel, the tailor, in the 2015 Broadway revival, **Adam Kantor** took a trip to Eastern Europe, where the show is set, to soak in the atmosphere and to try to recapture the world as Aleichem knew it. In "My Long Journey From Anatevka to *Fiddler* on Broadway," he addresses the author directly and writes: "It seems that scholars (or those who refer to themselves as such) agree that your Anatevka, **Sholom Aleichem**, is not a real place. It is a fictional town, they believe, perhaps based on an amalgamation of your villages outside Kiev."

Perhaps even more remarkable is a story that came to light in *The Times of Israel*, which published a report on March 29, 2016 with the headline, "In real-life Anatevka, Ukraine's Jewish refugees cling to tradition."

In part, the story explains, "Thanks to one rabbi's unique project for Jewish refugees from the east . . . the nascent community of Anatevka, a small village . . . sprang into existence six months ago . . . where 20 families are now building a future. Named after the fictional hometown of Tevye the Dairyman . . . Anatevka is a tribute not only to that town but to the real Jewish shtetls (hamlets) that dotted Eastern Europe before the Holocaust."

But back to business . . .

Ron Spivak: "Of course, it's been discussed ad infinitum that **Zero Mostel** gave his best performance in *Fiddler* on opening night. By the second night (it is said) he was already bored, and started ad libbing. Whereas other actors' performances often grew and deepened during a run, his became more and more about 'schtick.'"

One groundbreaking musical, **Rodgers & Hammerstein's** *Oklahoma!*, would have been the choice of **Joe Schuchman**. He wrote that it "changed forever the concept of musical theatre and hearkened back to a much simpler time as the nation was at war in Europe and the Pacific. To hear that music for the first time would have been amazing."

For **Candee Sheppard**, to whom I was married in the FSFCTG production of *Applause*, it would have been another R&H show, **Yul Brynner's** opening night in *The King and I*. I bet a lot of my friends are surprised I didn't name that as my favorite, too, but the lure of an emerging **Streisand** was just too great.

An assortment of other musicals received recognition. **Richard Skipper**, a professional entertainer for whom I stage managed about a dozen talk/variety shows that he hosted, mentioned a wish to go back to the night of January 16, 1964, when the original marathon run of *Hello, Dolly!* began.

In response, **Peter Filichia**, a celebrated author of multiple books on the theater, said, "Ironically, on that very night that **Channing** was opening, I was at the Shubert in Boston seeing *Funny Girl* and still have the ticket to prove it."

Cesar F. Sostre, whom I knew when we were teenagers in Puerto Rico and with whom I reconnected on Facebook a few years ago, didn't go back as far as most responders, citing *The Producers* as his show-of-choice. "I saw it on Broadway but not the original cast. Funniest show I've ever seen," he said.

The same show was also named by **Michael Brooks**, wishing he could have run into the show's creator, **Mel Brooks**, "who probably was in the theater that night."

Also selecting a relatively "new" musical was **Justin Michael**, one of my students who once agreed to wear a dress in front of the entire school in one of our school plays. He would like to have been on hand to hear **Betty Buckley** sing "Memory" for the first time in *Cats*.

While musicals received an overwhelming percent of the votes, several straight plays were represented, as well.

Bruce Levy, a long-time friend from my days on *Phoenix* who, like myself, took over as Arts Editor at the paper, mentioned "**Laurette Taylor** in *The Glass Menagerie*. I want to find out why this was considered one of the greatest performances of all time."

Rod Singleton, who starred as Coalhouse Walker in the FSFCTG production of *Ragtime,* on which I was one of the producers, would "turn back time to 1987 to the opening of *Fences* with **James Earl Jones**."

And, I must admit, I was flattered when **Brandon Maggart**, a Broadway veteran with countless credits to his name, offered his own insight, citing the opening of *Gypsy* as his most coveted ticket . . . with a twist. He would have chosen the London production that starred **Angela Lansbury**, prior to its arrival on Broadway as the show's first revival there.

Turning to a show in which he shared the stage with **Lauren Bacall** and **Len Cariou**, he confided that "For me personally, opening night of *Applause* was special. After only two (or three?) previews and then opening night, plus next day with the wonderful notices coming out, then the Tony nominations."

Understandable. Special, indeed.

[NOTE: According to the Internet Broadway Database, *Applause* actually played four previews, leading to its 896 regular performances.]

Chapter Sixteen

WHAT SHOW MOST PLEASANTLY SURPRISED YOU?

*S*ometimes, our pre-conceived notions can enhance or hinder our enjoyment of a particular show. If a show gets glowing reviews, or if friends rave about it, or if it seems to be constantly in the headlines, more often than not, when I go to see it, anticipating something that will live up to all the hype, I am left to wonder what all the hoopla was about. On the other hand, if all signs are negative, I'm quite often pleasantly surprised. Perhaps the best way to see a show is with a completely open mind, when it's in early previews, before word of mouth leaks out. Of course, nowadays, thanks to social media, people begin talking about a show, and predicting its failure or success, even before it gives its first public performance.

Back in the early '70s, I went to see an off-Broadway production of a new musical about which I knew absolutely nothing. I went in with a friend, who, similarly, had heard very little about it, other than, as he put it at the time, "It's supposed to be good."

What we saw was a little show called *Grease,* and we both had a most incredible time. It was loaded with songs that conjured memories of a bygone era. A parody of the 1950s, the show took an often hilarious look at a group of high school students inter-acting and trying to find themselves. As a college student at the time, I could still relate. With a focus on greaser Danny (guys were called that then because of the elaborate greasy coifs they sported on their heads) and Sandy, the girl of his dreams, there was romance—and game playing—aplenty.

And there was a cast of talented but relatively unknown actors, several of whom would go on to major careers, among them **Barry Bostwick** (who would win a Tony Award for Best Actor in a Musical for *The Robber Bridegroom*), **Adrienne Barbeau** (perhaps best known as **Bea Arthur**'s daughter on the long-running television situation comedy series, *Maude*), and **Walter Bobbie**, whose greatest fame would come as a Broadway director, most notably his Tony-winning work on *Chicago,* now the second longest-running show in Broadway history. And the original Sandy, **Carole Demas**, is now a personal friend.

Grease opened at the Eden Theatre in downtown Manhattan on February 14, 1972. I saw it a little over a week later, on February 23. An orchestra ticket went for $7.90.

One odd memory I have of that evening: As we entered the theater, the weather was just a typically cold New York City winter's day. When we emerged a couple of hours later, there must have been two or three inches of snow on the ground, coming, seemingly, out of nowhere. One fellow theatergoer, a woman behind us, took one look and gasped, "Oh, my God, and I'm wearing sandals!" The things we remember!

One of the first shows I reviewed in the Queens College
Phoenix newspaper.

As for the show itself, to call it a pleasant surprise would be an understatement. We loved it and I would eventually see it again —twice—after it moved to Broadway. Of course, it went on to a record-setting run, becoming, at the time, Broadway's longest-running show, eventually amassing the then-staggering total of 3,388 performances.

Reviewing it in the Queens College *Phoenix* newspaper, I wrote, "Just as *No, No, Nanette* revived present-day interest in the twenties, so this show will probably revive interest in the fifties. *Grease* is a fast-paced and entertaining new musical . . . " A couple of years later, I re-reviewed it, saying, "Of the new wave of revivals and newly-created productions based on bygone times, it is *Grease*, a kooky romp about high schoolers in the fifties, which seems destined for the longest run." Good call, if I have to say so myself!

So, what shows offered such pleasant surprises for my Facebook friends? Here's what some of them had to say on the matter. Note that more than one experienced the greatest pleasure not knowing anything about a particular show.

Richard Bergman: "Surprise for me was *The Boy From Oz.* I went during previews, didn't know who **Hugh Jackman** was or that it was about the life of **Peter Allen** and boy, did I enjoy it!"

Alice Goldman Kasten: "I think maybe *Billy Elliot.* I knew nothing about it going in except that it was supposed to be very good. Wow! Also have to add *The Curious Incident of the Dog in the Night-Time.* I really didn't want to see it, as I have an autistic grandson . . . and I did cry during a large chunk of it—but it was truly wonderful."

Judith Mermelstein: *"Jersey Boys.* I came expecting a jukebox musical and saw instead a marvelous and creative piece of theater. Surpassed expectations in every respect."

Russ Woolley: "*A Gentleman's Guide to Love and Murder*—might be in my top three fave shows."

The single-named **Stephan,** a performer and Art Deco specialist I met when I stage managed a show called *The Life and Art* *of Erte* for The Ziegfeld Society, an organization dedicated to the preservation of musical theater history: *"A Gentleman's Guide to Love and Murder* was my very first time seeing a show on Broadway. I was absolutely delighted by it. I mean, any show that opens with the chorus telling you to go home because it's just too gruesome is my kind of show."

Edward Santos, a Facebook friend since 2013 whom I have yet to meet face to face: *"Good For Otto.* It is a current off-Broadway play that I saw last week. Was not looking forward to it—three-and-a-half hours long. LOVED IT."

Marilyn Garfinkel: "Seeing **Daniel Radcliffe** and **John Larroquette** in a revival of *How to Succeed in Business Without Really Trying.* I never thought anyone could come close to **Robert Morse**'s performance as Ponty, but Radcliffe was amazing. And the chemistry he had with Larroquette was fantastic."

Virginia Blackert, a friend I met on Facebook and with whom I recently had a first telephone conversation: *"Rent.* I had this really negative attitude about someone having the audacity to screw around with *La Boheme.* Finally saw it in a wonderful theater in South Florida and all I could say to the friend who dragged me was, 'How could you have let me miss this until now?'"

Loria Parker: *"Hamilton,* which I knew would be good but it's genius-ly original and beautiful and BTW, the dancing and stagecraft design are not nearly mentioned enough."

Kevin Craig, who grew up in our local community theater circle to become a prolific actor, director, and teacher: "Wonderful Lincoln Center show called *Happiness.* Saw it spur of the moment and it was terrific. Unfortunately, there was never a cast recording, though a few songs appear on YouTube from time to time."

Joe Schuchman: "The 1975 revival of the **Eugene O'Neill** play, *All God's Chillun Got Wings*, starring **Trish Van Devere** and **James Earl Jones** at Circle in the Square. Awful reviews, wonderful production."

Bill Logan: "*Follies*. The original production. Went to the first preview. Had no idea my world was about to be changed forever."

Chapter Seventeen

AND THE WINNER IS...

*T*he Tony Awards were named in memory of **Antoinette Perry**, an actress and director who founded a training center for performers. They have been handed out every year since 1947 for distinguished achievement in the theater, and are considered by many the highest honor a stage performer can receive.

Over the years, rules and even categories have changed. One particularly interesting point has to do with billing. The placement of performers' names over the title of a show automatically places them in the leading categories, but below-the-title billing, even if it's for leading roles, places them in the featured categories. However, four times each year, the Tony nominating committee meets to determine if there are to be any exceptions to the rule. There are usually several each year who end up in the more appropriate category. And there's the case of **Julie Andrews** who requested the withdrawal of her nomination for *Victor/Victoria* in protest over the other people involved in the show—both on stage and off—being completely overlooked, an oversight Miss Andrews famously referred to as "egregious." That move most likely cost her the Tony, which ultimately went to **Donna Murphy** for a revival of *The King and I*, blocking Miss Andrews' path to becoming an EGOT winner—Emmy, Grammy, Oscar, and Tony Awards, the ultimate show business accolade.

There are those who believe that such awards are intrinsically wrong. One week, I posed the following question: "Should performers compete against each other for awards?" Some interesting responses resulted.

I, for one, suggested, "I see nothing wrong with it. I think most people are naturally competitive and everyone enjoys recognition. So, what's the harm?"

Richard Skipper: "NO. How do you compare an apple to an orange?"

Kevin Craig: "I'm all for competition, though I sometimes find the winners to be arbitrary or not related directly to talent. I'd like to see the rubric for deciding the final votes."

Debbie Vogel: "My motivation when I perform is to express something about the human condition. The purpose of theater is not only entertainment, but also to be able to put ourselves in another person's shoes and have empathy. Who cares about a Tony? Participation in theater is its own reward."

Tamara Derieux: "I'd like to think that as artists they strive for SELF!"

Larry Bloom: "Competing for prizes and giving awards for 'Best of . . .' has been a tradition for decades! It also is essential for ticket sales, whether in theater, movies . . . I'm all for it as long as it's fair!"

JK Larkin: "Awards are great for the sake of marketing campaigns. I am a fan . . . as the speeches provide a phenomenal outlet for theater artists to speak on behalf of their work. However . . . I think that competition has a great potential to cause negative effects upon the people competing . . . This has proven in many circuits to be a detriment to the art more so than a celebration of the work."

Andrew Dinan: "We compete all the time insofar as when we see someone up their game, we are inspired to up ours. Notice how many times so-so actors and even very good actors upped their game when working with **Olivier**."

Mitchell Kessler: "They compete for roles, so . . . "

Joe Riley: "I have no problem with the competition. The fanfare attracts more attention to the arts (particularly theater) and I believe more attention is needed."

Joseph Schweigert: "I don't believe actors should have any interest in awards. Of course, it's nice to receive one or even be nominated for one; however, it should not be the primary motivation for what you set out to do. Remember, the play's the thing."

Candee Sheppard: "It's got to be really nice to get recognition for a job well done. I don't know. Do you think that actors perform just to win an award? If a performance is great, it's probably not the raison d'etre!"

Lloyd Baum: "I was in a one-act play competition in high school. I was a junior and won best actor, but we lost best play to the senior class. I had mixed emotions at the cast party. But I still have the trophy."

Michele Gerrig Newmark: "I think actors should give their all at every performance and embrace awards should they be given."

Michael Brooks: "I feel good, honest competition is exciting and only can enhance some performances, although it should not be the prime consideration."

Tommie Gibbons: "I thought they competed by working, doing their best work, and letting other people decide."

Chapter Eighteen

ONE SINGULAR MOMENT

*M*ost theater fanatics can clearly remember the show that first drew them to this magical world of ours. For many, like myself, that show would remain a personal favorite forever. And it is quite likely that each theater-goer can point to one particular moment in a show—be it part of their favorite or not—that stands apart from all the rest.

With this in mind, I posed the question on Facebook, "What single moment in a show absolutely thrilled, amazed, or in any other way, delighted you?"

For me, the one that stands above the rest happened at New York's Shubert Theatre, that beautiful Broadway jewel that first opened its doors on October 2, 1913.

This is how I described it on my page: "I remember seeing *A Chorus Line* for the first time and being amazed at the opening moment . . . the house went dark and in a nanosecond, the lights came up to reveal the entire cast on stage. I knew I was in for a great ride that night!"

A great ride, indeed. That first visit happened well into the show's nearly 15-year record-breaking run, but it would not be my last. In fact, I would see the show twice more before it would go dark for the last time on April 28, 1990, after 6,137 performances.

But that original thrill was never again to be duplicated for me. Perhaps the lights didn't come back up quite so quickly, or perhaps my familiarity with the show removed the element of surprise that undoubtedly played a large part in my initial feeling of awe. Sometimes we just have to accept that "one singular sensation," to quote an **Edward Kleban** lyric in the show, can only be truly experienced once.

Many others responded to my question, making for a kaleidoscope of unforgettable moments.

Javier Adrian Sanchez, a former student of mine who played Oscar Madison in our school's production of *The Odd Couple*, recalled that "in *The Lion King*, during the 'He Lives In You' reprise, the moment that Mufasa reappears as a cloud" stands out in his mind. "It was just a great, unexpected moment when everything came together perfectly—lights, costumes, music, dance, movement."

The same show also contained that special moment for **Larry Bloom**, with whom I attended a performance. As he put it, "The one moment that stands out above the others is the opening when the cast sang 'The Circle of Life' and the actors, costumed as animals, entered. Those minutes took my breath away!"

Opening moments of a show often pack the greatest wallop, as corroborated by **Gary Tifeld**, who remembered his experience at the original production of *42nd Street* in 1980: "It was less than two weeks after the infamous opening night where **David Merrick** announced **Gower Champion**'s passing at the curtain call. The reviews were outrageous and it was the hottest ticket in town. Like *Hamilton* hot. The anticipation was off the charts. Everyone in that theater felt so lucky and privileged to be there. Then the overture started . . . and when the curtain started to rise (slowly) to the sight and sound of those THOUSANDS of maniacally tapping feet . . . I and everyone else in that theater lost our freakin' minds!!! I've seen many great shows with thrilling moments since then, but no amount of chandeliers or helicopters will ever top that."

Show Boat, which has been mentioned by several friends as the one they would most have wanted to see on opening night, also provided THE magical moment for at least one of them. For **Bruce Bider**, it happened at the Jones Beach Theater, where he had been brought to see shows since childhood, "when the actual two-deck paddle wheeler that was built for this production came sailing into view to dock during the overture, and later on in the show when the boat 'opened up' for the interior scenes in the kitchen and auditorium. There will never again be anything like the grandeur of those Jones Beach shows."

Gary Eisele, who was working on a show at BroadHollow, a theater company on Long Island, many years ago, was duly impressed with one particular moment in it: "The opening of the stage being completely bathed in miniature lights emblazoned across the back of the stage was a stunning opening. Nothing quite like it since."

The stage setting was also the thing for **Stephan**: "In the original production of *Follies* when the 'Loveland' set appeared, it just knocked my socks off. Also, one little moment in *Sunday in the Park with George*, when the characters in the painting bow to him. I lose it every time."

Michele Gerrig Newmark mentioned the same show: "The first act finale of *Sunday in the Park with George* gives me goose bumps every time I see it—at least three times."

Candee Sheppard: "The first thing that comes to my mind was the nude scene in *Hair*. Being a young innocent, I didn't know there was one and I nearly jumped out of my seat. I actually exclaimed, 'Oh, my God, they're naked,' to the audience's amusement."

Mitchell Kessler chose a more contemporary moment: "In *Dear Evan Hansen*, **Ben Platt**, overcome by fear and shame, sat alone on stage, facing the audience, and without a word, began to tremble, slush, sweat and cry until he was a quivering heap of human flesh onstage. The sequence took a minute. Never saw anything like it."

Chapter Nineteen

ETHEL MERMAN AND OTHER CELEBRITY ENCOUNTERS

*I*n case you couldn't guess, I am star struck.

I've waited at many a stage door at the conclusion of a performance, hoping to catch a glimpse of the performers.

Heck, I've waited at many a stage door even when I hadn't just seen the show. In passing, I'd see a bunch of people gathered in front of one of the Broadway theaters and race over to find out who everyone was waiting for. Most of the time, I'd dart into the theater, pick up a Playbill, and join the crowd.

In those days, a much more innocent time and long before security was so tight, it was relatively easy to enter a theater, as well as most everywhere. How else could so many of us have "second-acted" so many shows without ever getting into trouble?

Those like us who hung around theaters used to be known—way before my time—as "stage door Johnnies," a term going back to the early 1900s. Back then it specifically referred to men who spent a lot of time at a theater in the hopes of gaining the romantic attention of an actress.

Our intentions were less lofty. If we were lucky, we'd come away with a photo or two with our favorite celebrities and, perhaps, some new autographs to add to our collections.

This calls to mind a man who was known all around the Broadway theater district in the 1970s. He appeared to be middle-aged, was always disheveled, and walked around with stacks of autographs, mostly on index cards, that he had amassed over the years.

He would walk up to someone—innocent people just walking up or down the street included—and ask if he or she was in show business. He didn't care who they were or how famous they might have been. If they were even remotely connected to the theater, he wanted their autographs.

He seemed to be everywhere, all the time. Autograph hunting appeared to be his full-time occupation. I overheard many a conversation between him and a star as he approached for an autograph. "Oh, come on, you must have me about six times already," they would say, or something close to that. It didn't matter. He would insist on yet another and they usually obliged. And, mind you, those were the days before people made a living selling this sort of thing on eBay!

But I digress—again! I've had many memorable experiences "stage dooring," and not just at Broadway shows. I spent more than a few summer afternoons during my high school and college years attending tapings of the television shows that were based in New York.

The David Frost Show, a syndicated talk series that ran from 1969 to 1972, was taped at what was then known as The Little Theatre, the name still visible on the building's 44th Street facade. It was later to be renamed for the first lady of the American theater, **Helen Hayes**, after the original theater bearing her name, two blocks away on 46th Street, was torn down in 1982, along with the Morosco and the Bijou, to make way for a new hotel, the New York Marriott Marquis.

I spent most of my vacation from school attending tapings of the show, which featured many well-known stars of the day, including **Julie Andrews**.

She happened to be the guest on Frost's birthday and in a pre-planned surprise for him, the audience joined Miss Andrews in singing "Happy Birthday" to him. I still refer to this as the time I sang with **Julie Andrews** on national television!

Unfortunately, I was unable to get Miss Andrews' autograph on that occasion, but I did meet up with her years later—the date was October 11, 1999—at the Barnes & Noble bookstore on Broadway at 66th Street for a book signing for her then-new children's publication, *Little Bo, The Story of Bonnie Boadicea*. Inside the front cover she signed her name as "**Julie Andrews Edwards**," her last name taken from her husband, film director **Blake Edwards**.

A welcome letter given out to patrons at the time reads in part, "**Julie Andrews Edwards** will only be signing books at today's event. She will not be able to sign memorabilia. Due to time constraints, **Julie Andrews Edwards** will not personalize your books today. She will only sign them. The taking of photographs is strictly prohibited at this event. Enjoy the signing!"

Well, despite all the restrictions, I had a great time. I had been thinking for days what I could possibly say to Julie. As I approached the desk, book extended, I said, "I have so many things I'd like to say to you, but I'll just say it's a pleasure to meet you."

To this, Julie, in her perfectly clipped British accent, replied, "It's a pleasure to meet you, too."

And with that, I was on my way.

I first met (to use the term loosely) **Ethel Merman**, often referred to as the first lady of the American musical stage, on July 25, 1970, the day I saw my first Broadway show, *Hello, Dolly!*

With a dozen hit shows behind her dating back to the 1930s, Miss Merman was nearing the end of her theatrical stage career. I am so fortunate to have been able to catch her before she took her final Broadway bow a few months later.

Miss Merman had been playing the title role since March of that year, following in the shoes and feathered hat of a long list of stars who had kept the show going into its seventh year, a record many at the time thought would never be broken.

I enjoyed the entire show, but I remember most vividly the scene in the Harmonia Gardens restaurant when Dolly was seated at a small round dining table downstage right, carving up some turkey for her intended, Horace Vandergelder. As she ate, she offered a bite or two to the theater patrons seated in the front row. How I wished she had done so to me, but as I was sitting up in row E, seat 111 of the balcony, that was not the least bit likely. Still, I loved how she broke that proverbial fourth wall, making me feel we were all in this together.

After the show, I waited for Miss Merman at the stage door. As I recall, she came out and headed straight for her waiting limousine, barely acknowledging the fans who had gathered on the sidewalk outside the St. James Theatre.

I walked up to the closed window of the limo and, with my Playbill in hand, indicated to Miss Merman that I wanted her to sign it for me. Through the glass she motioned to me, perhaps even mouthing the words, "I'm sorry," looking as if she really meant it, as the car joined the traffic heading off on 44th Street.

But this would not be the last time Miss Merman and I would come face to face. As you are finding out, I don't give up getting an autograph that easily. Years later, in 1978, Miss Merman wrote a book about her life, entitled simply, *Merman: An Autobiography*. Naturally, when I heard there was to be a book signing, I immediately planned to attend.

The exact date and place elude me, perhaps because I was otherwise preoccupied at the time . . . planning my approach. I was just two or three years out of school, working for pittance at a publishing company while awaiting an appointment to begin my teaching career, and money was tight. I knew I couldn't buy the book that day, but that wasn't what I was aiming for.

Armed with a couple of her old vinyl recordings, the original cast album of the Lincoln Center production of *Annie Get Your Gun* and one of her solo albums, "Ethel's Ridin' High," a collection of show tunes by the likes of **Cole Porter**, the **Gershwins**, and **Bock & Harnick**, which was released in 1974, I headed into the city, as we outer-borough residents refer to Manhattan.

The line was, not surprisingly, long, giving me ample time to review the situation and to figure out the best approach. I knew she wasn't supposed to sign any memorabilia, especially for anyone not buying the book, but I figured I would explain my predicament and hoped she would be sympathetic.

My turn finally arrived. I reached into my shopping bag and took out the two record covers (I would never bring along the actual records on excursions such as this). Not wanting anyone except Miss Merman to hear my story, I placed the albums on the L-shaped table in front of her, leaned over, and moved in a bit closer to her to whisper my explanation.

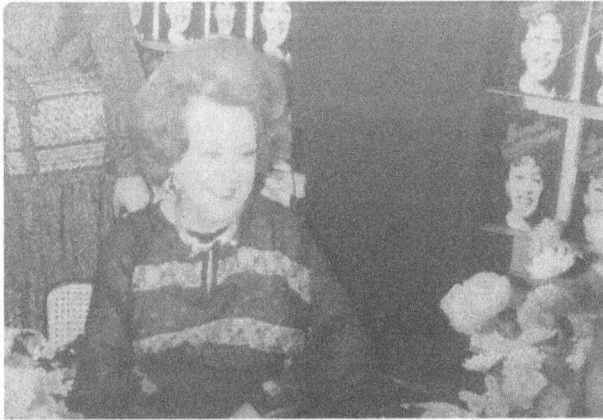

The day Ethel Merman called security on me. But she did sign my album covers!

I don't think I got a single word out before that famous stentorian voice filled the entire department.

"Security! Security! This man is trying to get behind the table."

Within seconds, security was on the scene, assessing the situation. I, of course, was totally humiliated. Not only would everyone now know I wasn't buying the book, but I caused Broadway's biggest star to have a near breakdown.

"No, no," I assured her and the guards, whispering my explanation, "I can't buy the book today and I only wanted to ask Miss Merman to sign a couple of my records."

Everyone seemed to agree I posed no clear and present danger, and Miss Merman graciously signed both album covers. The writing implement of choice was a magic marker, not always the wisest option for writing on glossy covers. The "E" in Ethel, in fact, smeared on one of them, either at the time or sometime after that.

But I got my **Ethel Merman** autographs. It may have taken eight years, but mission finally accomplished.

I got my autograph!

Of course, friends of mine have many a memorable tale to tell about their own encounters with celebrities, which they shared with me—and the world—on Facebook.

Bruce Levy pointed out that he was with me the day I caused Miss Merman to have a panic attack.

"I still have the signed book," he wrote in response to my online question. "I presented her with my *Happy Hunting* program to sign and said, 'This is for you, too.' She replied, 'Oh, no honey, I've got that already,'" obviously mistakenly believing he was presenting her with a gift. According to Bruce, the signing happened in, of all places, the linen department at Bloomingdale's, a detail I had long forgotten.

Mitchell Kessler related this story: "A couple of years ago, I took my son, Matt, to see *Waiting for Godot* with **Ian McKellen** and **Patrick Stewart**. In another world, they are both stars of the X-Men movies and McKellen was also in *Lord of the Rings*, all of which Matt loves. Both men came out for autographs. The great Gandalf [McKellen's on-screen alter ego] is just a sweet little old man. McKellen had a technique for getting up against the barricade and putting his arm around you so it looks in your photo like you're standing next to each other on the street. He did that with Matthew. I snapped the picture."

Alison Feuer Pascuzzi: "When I saw *Hairspray*, with **Harvey** [**Fierstein**, though some people just need a single name!], I saw **Nathan Lane** in the audience at intermission. I said, 'I love you,' and he said, 'I love you, too.' Then I told him I wanted to hug him and he opened his arms and we hugged—for several seconds."

Another cuddly moment no doubt pleased **Cecilia Vaicels**, with whom I've worked on several community theater productions: "When **Ben Vereen** was in *Fosse*, I waited for him at the stage door. I was so excited to meet him, I cried—sobbed, actually, and he put his arms around me and held me until I could compose myself."

Cesar F. Sostre: "Not sure this counts but saw **Philip Seymour Hoffman** sitting on a stoop outside the theater one New York morning. Did not approach him since he looked pissed off."

Edward Santos: "Met **Angela Lansbury** backstage during the tour of *Sweeney Todd* in Boston. Her husband, **Peter Shaw**, met me at the stage door and brought me to her dressing room. We entered just in time to hear her flushing the toilet. She was very lovely and signed my hardcover *Sweeney Todd* book."

This prompted **Bruce Bider** to respond, "How many people can say they heard **Angela Lansbury** flush the toilet?" Not that many, I would presume!

Of course, sometimes we meet people we admire under quite unusual circumstances.

From **Bill Logan**, another story about the five-time Tony Award-winner: "I guess my most memorable encounter was when I was in post-graduate school. I interviewed **Angela Lansbury** in her apartment at the Manhattan Plaza for an hour and a half. What an intelligent and gracious and kind person she is."

Judith Mermelstein: "Did I ever tell you my **Zero Mostel** story? I was at the reception desk at his lawyer's office. At the time, I was like a size three. He waltzed in and without breaking stride, scooped me up from behind the desk and carried me under an arm into his lawyer's office, announcing, 'I'd like to thank the Academy . . . '"

John O'Hare, a long-time member of our local community theater scene who directed me in a production of *A Funny Thing Happened On the Way to the Forum* at the Parkside Players, and generally a man of few words: "I met **Joel Grey** on the subway."

Larry Bloom: "I saw **Captain Kangaroo** and **Jackie Onassis** on a $59 flight from New York to Washington." Just for the sake of clarification, Larry went on to explain that they were on two different flights but with the same airline.

Michele Gerrig Newmark: "**Mako** [the Tony Award-nominated star of Broadway's original production of *Pacific Overtures*] was at a dinner party at the home of a mutual friend some years ago. He was witty, utterly charming, and down to earth."

Another memory from **Judith Mermelstein**: "I sat next to **Isaac Asimov** [the prolific science fiction writer] at a Gilbert & Sullivan Society meeting once. He had a lovely baritone. I was too shy to speak to him!"

Michele Gerrig Newmark had her own but similar encounter with the famed author: "Mr. Asimov sat behind me at a G&S meeting some years ago. As I recall, he didn't sing."

Rene Bendana, whom I've known for years from community theater: "While driving a limousine and waiting at American Airlines, another limo pulls up. Out step **Julie Andrews** and **Blake Edwards**. Mr. Edwards was infirm and needed extra help to exit his car. I obliged and Miss Andrews thanked me profusely. I said, 'If I knew you were coming I would've brought my resume.' She quipped, 'If I knew I would have brought mine!' We both laughed."

Chapter Twenty

IT'S TIME FOR ANOTHER LIST!

*M*y friends, as you have probably noticed, are a widely varied group, with lots of thoughts on every aspect of theater. To get a feel for their personal likes, I asked a question that I hope will give you some idea as to some plays you might want to check out for yourself: "Of the plays you have seen/read/been in, what is your favorite (a) musical, (b) drama, (c) comedy?"

For me, it would have to be: (a) *The King and I* (a no-brainer!), (b) *Death of a Salesman*, (c) *The Man Who Came to Dinner.* I'm still on the lookout for more modern plays that would offer me the same amount of pleasure.

Here were some of the responses I got:

Jack Taylor Macaluso: (a) *Cabaret,* (b) *'night, Mother,* (c) *The Women*

JK Larkin: (a) *Assassins,* (b) *The Humans,* (c) *A Doll's House, Part 2*

Candee Sheppard: (a) *Fiddler On the Roof*, (b) *The Diary of Anne Frank*, (c) *God's Favorite*

Bill Logan: (a) *Sweeney Todd*, (b) *August: Osage County*, (c) *Private Lives*

Alison Feuer Pascuzzi: (a) *Funny Girl*, (b) *The House of Bernarda Alba*, (c) *Lovers and Other Strangers*

Marilyn Garfinkel: (a) *Man of La Mancha*, (b) *Twelve Angry Men*, (c) *Harvey*

Erik Neilssen: (a) *Chicago*, (b) *A Few Good Men*, (c) *Noises Off*

Lloyd Baum: (a) *Les Miserables*, (b) *The Mousetrap*, (c) *Enter Laughing*

Sharon Weinman: (a) *Grey Gardens*, (b) *The Member of the Wedding*, (c) *You Can't Take It with You*

Michele Gerrig Newmark: (a) *Fiorello!*, (b) *The Crucible*, (c) *You Can't Take It with You*

Mitchell Kessler: (a) *South Pacific*, (b) *Death of a Salesman*, (c) *You Can't Take It with You*

Solomon Buchman: (a) *Les Miserables*, (b) *The Elephant Man*, (c) *Breaking Legs*

Joseph Schweigert: (a) *Man of La Mancha*, (b) *Twelve Angry Men*, (c) *Room Service*

Michael Brooks: (a) Tie: *Les Miserables* and *1776*, (b) *The Mousetrap*, (c) *A Funny Thing Happened On the Way to the Forum*

Joe Riley: (a) *Man of La Mancha*, (b) *Of Mice and Men*, (c) *Noises Off*

Miles Tepper: (a) Tie: *Fiddler on the Roof* and *West Side Story*, (b) Tie: *Death of a Salesman* and *A Raisin In the Sun*, (c) *You Can't Take It with You*

Debbie Vogel: (a) *Carousel*, (b) *A Streetcar Named Desire*, (c) *You Can't Take It with You*

Chapter Twenty-One

NOBODY'S PERFECT

*W*hile theater is wonderful, those who participate in it, no matter how talented and well-rehearsed they might be, are not infallible. That's part of what makes it the unique experience it is. At times, we witness something going wrong in a production or even commit an on-stage blunder of our own. So, one week I asked: (a) What imperfection(s) have you seen from the audience? (b) If you perform, what flub(s) of your own will you admit to?

To tell the truth, I posed similar questions twice, once back in 2012 and again six years later. Some friends participated both times, referring to the same incident on both occasions. I, however, shared different experiences each time. The first go-round, my mind turned to a play I had seen in 1976. It was presented by the Phoenix Theatre as part of its Festival of American Plays: A Bicentennial Celebration! at The Playhouse.

An insert in the Playbill reminds theatergoers that "It's not too late to subscribe! Your ticket stub saves you $3.00 on a subscription to the remaining 3 plays. Attach your stub (so we'll know which play you've seen) and deduct $3.00 from the subscription price of the series you choose. Order as many subscriptions as you like." It should be pointed out that a subscription to the theater's four-play season that year could be had for as little as $21.

As for The Playhouse, it was located at 359 West 48th Street, serving as a theater from 1970 to 1983. This theater is not to be confused with a similarly named one that was located nearby until it was demolished to allow for the expansion of Rockefeller Center.

Okay, Mark, let's get back on track. Here is how I answered my question in 2012:

"I was at 27 *Wagons Full of Cotton,* a little-known **Tennessee Williams** play featuring **Meryl Streep** before she became **Meryl Streep**. As I recall, she was talking about the heat and dryness as smoke started filling the theater. We all thought it was an effect —until they made us evacuate. A short while later, we were allowed back in, and they took the play from the top."

So early was this performance in her career that Streep had made only one previous appearance on Broadway the year before and had not yet made her film debut, which was still two years away. But her talent was already being recognized, earning her a nomination for a Tony Award for Actress in a Featured Role in a Play.

When I responded to a similar question last year, I answered thusly:

"I was at a performance of an off-Broadway play starring **Rosemary Harris**. She was in the middle of a dramatic scene with another actress when a light bulb directly above them popped, sending bits of glass all around. The audience gasped; the moment was temporarily lost; and then, somehow—magically, it seemed—with the slightest gesture, Ms. Harris got the scene back on track as if nothing untoward had happened."

As for my own imperfections on stage, I recalled that "I was in a production of *Two By Two*. I had a wonderful duet that contained one line near the end of the song that I always had trouble remembering. One night, as the song began, I had that line in the back of my mind, so as not to forget it. We were just a few notes into the song when that line came to the front of my mind and out of my mouth. I could see the music director flipping pages very rapidly to catch up and, just like that, the song was over. We got polite applause, with the audience probably thinking, 'Gee, that was a short song!' My co-star could not have been pleased, but I apologized profusely when we got off stage and she gracefully accepted."

Shana Aborn: "*Forum* revival. Toward the end of Act I, **Nathan Lane** (Pseudolus) was giving **Mark Linn-Baker** (Hysterium) the important prop ring. It slipped out of his hand and rolled right down into the crack between the apron and the orchestra platform. Gone. The two of them stared a minute, then burst into uncontrollable giggles for a good ten minutes. Every time they tried to get back into character, they started laughing again. Of course, the audience is howling, too. Lane starts joking with the crowd: 'Can you believe they gave me a Tony for this?' Never saw star actors lose it like that."

Ellen Weinstock Rosenberg, with whom I go way back in community theater productions: "Many years ago, I watched a performance of **Steve Lawrence** in *What Makes Sammy Run?* In the middle of a passionate speech he spat at one of the actresses right in the face. He stopped the whole show to apologize and kept asking her if she was all right. She assured that she was and the show continued on."

Gary Tifeld: "Second time seeing *Deathtrap*. **Robert Reed** was Sidney. Act I, Scene 1. He goes to the phone, picks up the receiver, dials, then picks up the phone and starts walking around with it as he's talking . . . but the receiver was not plugged in. So, he's walking around chatting away with the cord dangling freely. The audience is laughing. **Marian Seldes** has her head down, and he keeps talking obliviously. Finally, he notices, and the look on his face was worth whatever the tix cost. He plugged in the phone, gave a 'do-over' gesture to the audience, then started over."

Larry Bloom: "I was in a production of *Come Blow Your Horn* and the actress who played Aunt Gussie came out to say her one line three scenes too soon. As the director, I gave her a note about this for the next performance. So, at the next performance, the actress waited and waited until the performance was done. She had waited too long!"

Bill Logan: "Back in the mid-'60s, some local producer inexplicably brought in a community theater production of *Auntie Mame* from Corpus Christie to play the Houston Music Hall (at that time the largest professional venue in Houston, home to Broadway touring productions). My friend and I only made it to the end of the first party scene. The end of the scene comes. Mame says her final line (lit cigarette in long holder). Blackout. Only you could still see the lit end of her cigarette in the darkness. The ember starts to slowly move across the stage when all of a sudden it makes a rapid dive for the stage floor, followed by a loud thump and an even louder expletive from the actress. We had to leave immediately due to our hysterical laughing."

Tommie Gibbons: "I saw **Patti LuPone** mess up the lyrics to 'Mr. Goldstone' at City Center. Nobody was more surprised than she was."

Jack Carr: "In summer stock at the old Oquaga Lake, Liat and I were in the embrace at the end of 'Younger Than Springtime.' A blackout was scheduled to allow us to exit stage left. Didn't happen. That was one long embrace."

Those blackouts, or lack thereof, can really kill you. Another such story, from a different perspective:

Cecilia Vaicels: "I saw *On the Waterfront* during its very short run on Broadway. Tech didn't go to blackout at the end of a scene and, after waiting a long time, a supposedly dead body got up and walked off stage. God help me . . . I laughed out loud. Poor guy."

In fact, it's well-known that technical mishaps are often the most consequential.

Richard Grillo: "When I saw **Sutton Foster** in *Thoroughly Modern Millie,* she got into the elevator and it didn't work. Also saw *Beauty and the Beast* and the set didn't turn around. There was an announcement about tech difficulties and about 20 minutes till they resumed."

Another case in point:

Barbara Auriemma: "Broadway...*The Producers* . . . Upon exiting stage left, **Matthew Broderick** goes to open door and entire door comes off hinges . . . looking at **Nathan Lane** [yes, him again!] with a 'What should I do?' look . . . he eloquently took the door with him upon leaving."

And yet another:

Lloyd Baum: "I was at the **Alfred Molina** revival of *Fiddler on the Roof*. During 'The Dream,' they flew Motel and Tzeitel, upstage center. When Fruma-Sarah finished her curse, and all the ghosts left the stage, the lifting system froze and the two of them were left hanging for Tevye and Golde's duet."

Fredwin Palacio, who appeared in my production of *Sweet Charity* and with whom I shared the stage in *Broadway Around the World*, a musical revue: "I was in the audience at the City Center production of *Follies*, when the actress singing 'Broadway Baby' forgot her lyrics. She sang to the conductor, 'I'd like to go back' . . . to the tune of 'to Washington Heights.' We in the audience loved and cheered her on. She ended the song with a standing ovation. It's on YouTube if you'd like to see it."

Richard Allman: "Many years ago in Detroit, I was doing **The Gershwins'** *Girl Crazy*. There's a scene in a bar where I was supposed to have substantial dialog with a girl who failed to show up. I ended up ad-libbing a scene with the bartender. She never did enter, so I finally said goodbye to him and left."

Barbara Auriemma: "I was in a really bad production of *Company* many years ago . . . it was so bad I didn't tell anyone about it . . . midway during the first performance the cast realized that one ensemble scene had not even been blocked . . . it gave a whole new meaning to the word ad-lib. As a disclaimer, I did not direct this production."

Then there are moments when audience members inadvertently steal the show.

Bill Logan: "I was playing Tom in a production of *The Glass Menagerie*. There was a scene where I was out on the stoop and Amanda was supposed to come out from the living room to talk to me. The set designer had accidentally put a slip-lock door-knob on the set, and, sure enough, it locked one night during performance. Amanda couldn't get it open to save her life, becoming more and more agitated as she tried. Finally, one of her drunk relatives in the second row yells, 'Go 'round, Doris Ann.' She did and the scene continued."

Alice Goldman Kasten: "We were among the few people who saw the Broadway production of *Chu-Chem*. Saw a preview performance. Lights go off, music starts to play, we hear movement noises (sounds like dancing) from behind the closed curtain. Someone behind me yells, 'Are you going to lift the curtain?' Curtain finally goes up—people are dancing on a dark stage. Same man behind us yells, 'Are you going to turn on the lights?'"

Sometimes, missteps are no laughing matter. **John Baratta**, who has appeared on stage in many local productions, but more frequently can be found toiling away behind the scenes: "Was backstage moving sets around. One of the crew members bumped into a column. It fell over and hit an actor on the side of the head, cutting him in the ear."

As for any mistakes of his own, **Andrew Burke**, with whom I appeared in a wonderful local production of *The Sound of Music*, would say only this: "I admit to none. If covered well, that audience never knows. I'd like to keep it that way!"

Chapter Twenty-Two

TO EACH HIS OWN

A rather trivial but nonetheless, I think, interesting question to ponder: "What one piece of theatrical memorabilia would you like to own?"

I wrote: "I'd opt for the original 'blackboard' used in the 'Getting to Know You' scene of *The King and I,* fulfilling my love of both the show and teaching."

Here are some of the other coveted pieces of theatrical history friends would love to have, including some rather oversized ones:

Alvaro Rotondaro, a long-time friend: "Henry Higgins' library. It looks amazing."

Stephan: "The 'Loveland' set."

Neil Einleger: "The revolving door from *Grand Hotel* (since the 'Loveland' set was already claimed)."

Michele Gerrig Newmark: "The set of the recent *She Loves Me.* I'll settle for a cookie-jar replica whose exterior opens to reveal the parfumerie."

Marilyn Garfinkel: "I think it would be super cool to own the surrey with the fringe on top."

Ron Spivak: "**Richard Kiley**'s original corkscrew sword from *La Mancha.*"

Gary Tifeld: "Sweeney's barber chair. Not sure where I'd put it, but . . . "

Brad Reiter: "The chandelier and the mask from *Phantom of the Opera.*"

Solomon Buchman: "Two items: (1) The pair of silver candlesticks given to Jean Valjean by the Bishop of Digne in *Les Miserables*, and (2) The model of the church built by John Merrick in *The Elephant Man.*"

Larry Bloom: "The boson whistle that the Captain used in *The Sound of Music* to summon his staff and children."

Bill Logan: "Guido's conductor's baton from *Nine.*"

Barbara Auriemma: "The tally board from *1776.*"

Kathleen Hassett Hochberg: "The flower **Stephen Nathan** wore on his lapel in the original production of *Godspell.*"

Andrew J. Koehler, one of the younger members of our local community theater circle: "The original Elphaba broom in *Wicked.*"

Richard Skipper: "**Carol Channing**'s original Dolly gown from *Hello, Dolly!*"

JK Larkin: "Definitely a trombone from the original *Music Man*."

Cathy Bandin Chimenti, a frequent performer on stages on Long Island and Queens who, as of late, has turned to directing, as well: "Original dressing room table from *Funny Girl*."

Judith Mermelstein: 'I'll take the axe from *Noises Off*.'

Lloyd Baum: "The Golden Helmet of Mambrino."

Michael Brooks: "The sword (Excalibur) from *Camelot*. I would love it!"

Shana Aborn: "Milky-White. Or any of the *Lion King* masks."

Candee Sheppard: "Maybe Guinevere's crown."

Mitchell Kessler: "Probably **Robert Preston**'s band leader jacket as Harold Hill, or better, **Herschel Bernardi**'s vest as Tevye. I'd like to wear it."

And, finally . . .

Mike Beaury, another local actor who passed through the hallowed halls of Queens College: "**Kristin Chenoweth**."

Chapter Twenty-Three

THEATRICAL PET PEEVES, ANYONE?

a simple enough question but, boy, did it yield some interesting responses.

I, for one, dislike the practice of according a standing ovation to EVERY SINGLE show. In so doing, I believe it takes away from those standing O's that are REALLY deserved. It used to be that when an audience stood, it was to show appreciation for a truly outstanding performance . Nowadays, it's par for the course.

Many of my friends had plenty to say on things that vex them— from various theatrical vantage points.

Solomon Buchman: "Other actors offering unsolicited 'advice' or 'suggestions' to fellow performers. These tidbits usually turn out to be unhelpful and/or self-serving. Leave it to the director to direct his actors."

Sharon Weinman: "Long lines at the women's room. Not only should they have more toilets, but people should wear theater attire where they can pee quickly. What's the deal with freshening up and reapplying make-up. The actors don't care how you look."

David Arzberger, a multi-talented theatrical personality with whom I've never had the opportunity to work but who I've seen on stage many times: "Wear the costume you were given. I hate when actors complain about the costume they are given. Just wear what the director and designers envision."

Michele Gerrig Newmark: "People who carry on running conversations during overtures to musicals and who are obnoxious when they're shushed."

Bruce Bider: "ReviSals (i.e. *Annie Get Your Gun* and *Flower Drum Song*), and modern monkeying (i.e. the new ending to *My Fair Lady*) and the cutting of overtures."

John O'Hare: "Cast members going into the audience. Keep your butt on the stage."

Marilyn Garfinkel: "Lack of good quality listening devices and open captioned shows for people like me and my sister who have severe hearing loss . . . Too often they don't work well and at times they don't work at all. The latest devices are awesome— each individual gets a small screen so he or she can read the dialogue. I have yet to see that on Broadway, but some newer movie theaters have that option."

Jack Taylor Macaluso: "It irks me that after ALL THIS TIME we must be reminded via recording to turn off all our devices and simply watch the show that we all paid good bucks to see."

Barri Sperber Feuer, who performed as part of a traveling cabaret act I was in called *Music On Tour*, and whose children have more recently joined their mother in stage performances on Long Island: "Audience members that come late and have to be seated between songs in the middle of the show! And worse, the audience members that leave in the middle of curtain calls, or as the last scene is ending to 'beat the crowds' out of the theater. So rude—pisses me off!"

Tamara Derieux: "In dance, the impromptu ovation for a particular move generated by audiences who have no understanding of the craft. They clap for the 'spectacular' and have no idea of the amount of control, strength and discipline it takes to make and maintain a 'minor' movement."

Gary Eisele: "The dropping of the '4th wall.' Unless the show was specifically written that way, keep it in place."

Kyle P. Carter, a former student of mine whom I never knew had an interest in performing until much later, when I discovered he was a member of SAG/AFTRA, the professional actors' union: "Cliques among actors. Where performers alienate other actors to make them feel like they are not part of the ensemble."

Bill Logan: "Pre-recorded music tracks. Makes the whole show seem pre-recorded."

Melanie Lee: "I hate body mics. Actors should learn to project. Or mic the stage."

Gary Tifeld: "People who get up and leave during the curtain calls. That's like going to someone's home for dinner, then leaving without saying, 'Goodnight, thank you for having me.' Not to mention how rude and inconsiderate it is to the rest of the audience."

Perhaps the single most relatable response of all came from **Cameron Hughes**, an actor on our local community theater scene, who said simply, "The prices."

Chapter Twenty-Four

A QUESTION OF CASTING

Throughout my teaching career, I had the opportunity to direct many student productions, all of which, I think it accurate to say, featured actors and actresses who did not fit the authors' original descriptions. At August Martin High School, a public school with a couple thousand students, two or three of whom were not African-American, we had an all-black cast in *The Sound of Music*, including the Nazis. When we put on *Cabaret*, not only were the Nazis played by young black performers, so was Herr Schultz, who was supposed to be a German Jew. In *Raisin*, the musical based upon *A Raisin In the Sun*, the one white character, Karl Lindner, representing the Clybourne Park "Improvement Association," on a mission to dissuade the family from moving into the white neighborhood, was played by an African-American, though admittedly of lighter skin tone than most of his cast mates.

When I transferred to Robert F. Kennedy Community High School, another public school, but one with a student population that could match the United Nations in diversity, we had an Hispanic Oscar Madison and an Asian Felix Ungar heading the cast of *The Odd Couple*.

Strangely enough, or perhaps not, it never crossed my mind that there was anything wrong with any of this. And I don't think any of the actors gave it a second thought. We were a teacher and his students, all of us sharing a love of the theater, and we just had a great time putting on our productions. And, judging from the enthusiastic response from our audiences, it seems they were willing to suspend their disbelief as they came along with us for the ride.

Of course, a school setting, much like community theater, is a special situation, and I don't particularly advocate casting against type just for its own sake. I find the custom particularly jarring in professional settings, where there are enough actors of every sort and variety to cast roles as originally intended.

As of late, it seems every show includes at least one example of "blind" casting, either in terms of race, or sex, or physical limitations. It seems, in fact, to have become de rigueur, something of a statement, a necessity in order to be viewed as current. It also seems to have become a topic of controversy. So, one week, on Facebook, I asked: How do you feel about this apparent trend?

"As one who has done it," I wrote, "I would have to say in some cases it's fine, but when it's done for shock value or just to be 'modern,' not so much. There are certain iconic roles and very specific character types with whom it just doesn't work."

As expected, reactions were varied and swift.

Larry Bloom: "For the most part, I think it works! Look at **Whoopi Goldberg** in *Forum*. Look at the role of Carrie in

Carousel a few years ago; **Audra McDonald** made it her own! In the current revival of *Carousel,* **Joshua Henry** portrays Billy Bigelow . . . brilliantly, I understand."

Michele Gerrig Newmark: "He is, indeed, brilliant."

Melanie Lee: "I take it you mean color blind casting, or casting that breaks the character's physical type. I had the pleasure of playing Fruma-Sarah in a production of *Fiddler On the Roof* and I got excellent feedback. Another black woman played Grandma Tzeitel. I had a blast playing Fruma-Sarah and I think the audience enjoyed it, too. Of course, some cross-racial casting can be awkward, such as **Audra McDonald** playing the Beggar Woman in *Sweeney Todd* when you know her back story calls for another look. I also saw a Latino boy playing Riff in *West Side Story*. Now there's a black man playing Billy Bigelow (on Broadway), which casting could evoke echoes of Scary Black Man stereotypes. However, those stories are so well known that one can mentally jump over the hurdle of cross-casting and enjoy the performance. Such casting can also increase opportunities for actors who need them. Also, we've seen plenty of the reverse: white people playing Maria in *West Side Story*, King Mongut in *The King and I,* Madame Butterfly, et al. Such casting is more frowned-upon these days for various reasons—inauthenticity, lack of opportunity for performers of color. Yet, it still happens, and I don't think it should stop entirely, especially on the amateur level."

JK Larkin: "I think it's important to practice whenever possible. So much of classical theater was written before it was socially acceptable to be telling the stories of non-Caucasians and because of this, in order to break this, we as theater creators should seize the opportunity to show the progress of society."

Debbie Vogel: "As an actress, I love this. On a SAG [Screen Actors Guild] voucher, when it asks for race, I put HUMAN. However, for shows that are dealing with the struggles of minorities, it doesn't work. Prime example: *A Raisin In the Sun*."

Melanie Lee: "I'm picturing an all-white production of *A Raisin In the Sun*! I suppose if you live in an all-white community and you're a school or a local amateur theater company and you really want to do this . . . and do you darken your faces or not (probably not!) . . . "

Candee Sheppard: "Some roles don't work with a Caucasian person playing a black person and I think casting race-appropriate should happen all the time. I don't know about cross-gender. I find it distracting. I also feel casting people who are way too old for a part shouldn't happen."

Tracey Berse Simon: "What is comes down to is appropriateness to the story. Do not do color blind casting if you're depicting a husband and wife in the pre-Civil Rights era, e.g., he's white, she's black, unless that is what the story is about. Do not do color blind casting if being of a specific ethnic group is integral to the story, especially in historical plays. No black actors auditioned for my local theater guild's production of *You Can't Take It with You*, so my director asked me and another white actor to play Reba and Donald. I asked him if we could play the parts as Cubans, which would be appropriate since Cuba is mentioned in the play. He thought about it, but since the actor playing Donald couldn't do anything other than a **'Mel Blanc** Mexican' accent, we had to do it with Southern accents. Let's face it— neither really would've worked, but we did it anyway. There was a lot of blowback when **Jonathan Pryce** played a Eurasian in *Miss Saigon*. Would you do *Pacific Overtures* with a non-Asian cast? Interestingly, one of the best casting choices I saw was a **Rebel Wilson**-type playing the lead in *Bells Are Ringing*. Not only was she talented, but she gave a different dimension to her character—a fear of being seen by her crush because she was not traditionally attractive. It didn't have to be said. You just knew it."

Judith Mermelstein: "My daughter played Marcellus Washburn (as a guy) in her junior-high *The Music Man* and Charlie the salesman was also played by a girl (as a guy). The audience reaction when Kat took off her cap at curtain calls and let her waist-length hair fall when she bowed was classic. I think younger urban audiences who have seen their school and camp drama productions cast diversely and cross-gender are more accepting of seeing untraditional casting in classic roles. I remember **Joe Papp** [founder of the New York Shakespeare Festival] caught a lot of flak for doing it with **Shakespeare** but don't remember much fuss when **Pearl Bailey** took over the role of Dolly Levi. But my fave legend is that the role of the Leading Player [in *Pippin*] supposedly was written for an older white dude; nevertheless, a young **Ben Vereen** auditioned and changed the producers' concept of the role."

[**Pearl Bailey** was seen by some to be a casting stunt by producer **David Merrick**, but she and the all-black company kept the show running for an extra year or two, to much acclaim. It was said—perhaps facetiously—at one point that Merrick was considering having comedian **Jack Benny** play Dolly. Now, that would have been an idea ahead of its time!]

Erik Neilssen: "I place the character above the actor. That is to say that no matter the race or gender, does the actor/actress give me what I need as a director to tell the story? On the amateur level, we have to bend to this rule more than on the professional level. I would prefer to see a talented actress 'pants' a role before I see my neighborhood mailman struggle to deliver his lines, just because he is a man. Nothing against mailmen. Secondly, I put relationship and chemistry with other actors before race and gender, as well. If we change a gender of one character because they read well, what does that do to the rest of the relationships on stage? Do they have the appropriate chemistry to tell a love story? I have seen plenty of shows where this mark was missed completely. But it's not about their skin or gender; it's about what they bring to the part and the stage. On the professional level (and some amateur productions), if you get a fantastic turnout at auditions, you may get to make interesting choices to tell your story. I strongly adhere to the rule that a director should stay true to the story (what is written on the page) while making it their own. If within that margin they can make creative casting choices, I think that should be encouraged."

Kelsey Elizabeth Edquist, who owns Royal Princess Prep Party Company and also performs on local stages: "I think that as long as race has no bearing on the actual role itself, it's all right. For instance, to cast a man or woman of color in a show like *Wicked* seems completely reasonable to me, whereas to cast a white person as Coalhouse in *Ragtime* or any of the Asian roles in *King and I* poses an issue because the whole point of those shows is to bring to light how the characters in those time periods treated other races."

Debbie Vogel: "I was cast as one of the King's wives. It helped me understand different cultures and time periods. I did have Asian make-up and a black wig. It made me think about what it would be like to be one of many wives."

Michele Gerrig Newmark: *"Rothschild and Sons* at the York [an off-Broadway theater in Manhattan] a couple of years ago had VERY diverse casting. It worked."

Barbara Auriemma: "When I did *1776* as a gender blind production, my women took on the roles of men. They did not pretend to be women. In color blind casting, you are not asking a black performer to pretend he/she is white or a white person to pretend he/she is black. You are asking to not see color at all and most of the time it actually works. I don't particularly care for color blind casting in historically accurate productions . . . no matter what the 'primary' color is. On a lighter note . . . there is an Asian production of *Hairspray* on YouTube. When the cast appears on stage together, you cannot tell the white roles from the black."

Judith Mermelstein: "I think a mono-race production of *Hairspray* might be problematic in that race is a big plot point: The white characters could indeed be Asian but I can't see the black characters as anything but black. But I saw a production of *The Glass Menagerie* many years ago at York College [a branch of City University of New York], which is a predominantly black school. The actor playing Tom was white, in fact blond; but everyone else in the cast, including the actors playing his mother and sister, was black. And it totally worked."

Putting it most simply, **Michael Brooks** said: "Talent should always be the prime consideration! I see no problem!"

Chapter Twenty-Five

MY TWO WORLDS . . . AND ALEC BALDWIN

I've always tried to infuse my love of theater into my teaching, regardless of the subject, in the hopes that it might pique the interest of someone sitting there in front of me. For the most part, I taught English, so it usually wasn't too hard to find a way to justify my curriculum.

I would invariably include plays among the works of literature we would read, some of my favorites being *The Glass Menagerie, A Raisin In the Sun, Twelve Angry Men,* and, for a lighter mood, any of several of **Neil Simon**'s works. I even found occasions to include a musical or two. In the early 1980s, *Evita* was one of the biggest hits on Broadway, and I knew its central characters and some of the salty language would be appealing to my students. So, I did a cut-and-paste with the lyrics from the album (vinyl was still in vogue back then!), and that became our text for a while. As I have always felt plays are written to be acted, often-times, I would have students read at least parts of them aloud.

In the case of *Evita*, the original Broadway cast recording brought the show into our classroom.

One time, we were reading **Arthur Miller**'s *Death of a Salesman*, perhaps my absolute favorite play. No spoiler alert needed here: The leading character, Willy Loman, a salesman struggling to make ends meet while dealing with complex family issues and his own mental stability, dies, bringing the play to a tragic conclusion.

Near the end, Willy's devoted wife, Linda, appears at his gravesite, unable to understand why he would have taken his own life, especially just as things were starting to look brighter for the family. She addresses him as if he were standing in front of her, telling him that, at long last, the mortgage on their home, a major weight on Willy's shoulders, is finally paid in full. She breaks down sobbing.

As we were reading this scene aloud in class, it seemed everyone was very touched by the events and the beauty of Miller's language. Then I noticed one young man, seated in the first row at the stage right side of the room (if I were the audience at the front desk), turned his back to the rest of us and was struggling to stifle his laughter. I was furious. And let down. And disappointed. How could anyone possibly find anything funny about what we were reading? I wasn't about to cause a scene by calling him out on it in front of the class, and I certainly didn't want to disrupt the mood, which, except for his reaction, was totally apropos. I silently and casually approached the young man's desk, with none of the other students even aware that I had done so, so deeply involved were they in the reading. I tapped him on the shoulder. He turned toward me and I was stunned. Tears were streaming down his face and he was embarrassed to let anyone—especially any of his peers—see him in this emotional state. Right then and there I learned an important lesson about the power of theater. (More on its amazing powers follows in the next chapter.)

Another time, it was actually Mr. Simon's *Broadway Bound* that had a similar effect on another student. We were out on a class trip to see the play on Broadway, with **Joan Rivers** having taken over the role of the mother in a story based on Simon's own life and early career. Near the end of the play, the two young men in the play, representing Simon and his brother, Danny, also a writer of renown, primarily on television, have both moved out of their mother's home.

One of my students, sitting next to me, turned to me and, doing his best to hold back the tears, said, "That's so sad. Now she's all alone." Again, I was astounded by the ability theater had to touch the heart.

I don't know if either of those two young men (who, by now, likely have families of their own) took a further interest in theater, but I would like to think they did. And nothing would make me happier than to know that it was because of something I did.

For some of my classes, I was able to join forces with Broadway companies, like the Roundabout Theatre Company and the too-short-lived National Actors Theatre, that would send teaching artists out to the participating schools for weekly visits as part of semester-long residency programs. On such occasions, I would always "warn" potential students that this was going to be an English class "with a theatrical component," allowing for more extensive tweaking of the traditional curriculum. Sometimes students would be intrigued and sign up for it; other times they would decide it wasn't for them. You win some, you lose some. But when it came to getting young people interested in theater, I always did my best to succeed...and frequently did!

Those special classes would always include multiple trips to the theater. One semester, I had taken a class to see the revival of *Twentieth Century* on Broadway. Produced by the Roundabout Theatre, it starred **Alec Baldwin** and **Anne Heche**. We all had a wonderful time at the theater, but it was what happened later on that sticks out most in my mind . . . providing one of my all-time favorite theatrical stories.

I need mention that as part of the class, the students had to research what I called "theater luminaries," people who had made significant contributions to the theater. Names they could choose included the likes of **Harold Prince, Ethel Merman, Tennessee Williams, Stephen Sondheim, Richard Rodgers, Irving Berlin, Helen Hayes, Bob Fosse, Agnes DeMille, George Abbott** . . . top tier artists, each and every one. After learning about them, they would have to share their findings with their classmates in the form of oral presentations.

We spent quite a while on this project, at the conclusion of which there was an exam and, sad to say, the class did not do well. At all.

I was completely disheartened. I remember saying to the class, "Anyone with any interest at all in the theater would know every single name on that list."

To this, one student blurted out, "I bet even **Alec Baldwin** wouldn't know them."

A light bulb went off in our heads. Let's find out, we decided. Let's write to him and see.

Tommy Thorsen, on behalf of himself and his classmates, composed the following letter:

Dear Mr. Baldwin:

Hello, Mr. Baldwin. I am a student at Robert F. Kennedy High School. I am writing to you on behalf of my drama class, which is participating in the Roundabout Theatre's Page to Stage Program this semester. We recently saw *Twentieth Century,* and we wanted to thank you for taking the time after the performance to talk with us.

As part of our class, our teacher, Mr. Lord, recently gave us an exam on theatre "luminaries" who have played important roles in the history of the theatre. Our class, unfortunately, performed rather dismally on the test. Our teacher tried to make us, as theatre students, understand the importance of knowing about these individuals. He claimed, rather harshly, that if he pulled in ten strangers off the street they probably would have done better on the exam than we did. He claimed that anyone working in theatre would be familiar with the history of the individuals on his list.

I suggested we put his words to the test and, as we enjoyed seeing you recently, selected you to help us out.

Enclosed is a copy of the test. We would be very grateful if you could please take the test (at least parts I and II), completely unassisted, and using only your own knowledge of theatre history, and return the results to us. The outcome of your exam may sway our teacher to be more lenient on our grades.

We realize you may be very busy due to your schedule, but we would greatly appreciate it if you would take a small amount of time to complete the test. Thank you for your time.

Sincerely,

Tommy Thorsen and Classmates

The letter was signed by the students and off it went. Would we ever hear back from Mr. Baldwin? Time alone would tell.

As I recall, it took about three weeks, but we finally did get a response. Alec diligently filled in his name and the date—May 10, 2004—on the lines at the top of the exam paper. He completed parts I and II—the short answer sections, though he opted out of the essays in part III.

April 15, 2004

Mr. Alec Baldwin
c/o Roundabout Theatre Company
American Airlines Theatre
227 West 42 Street
New York, New York

Dear Mr. Baldwin:

Hello, Mr. Baldwin. I am a student at Robert F. Kennedy High School. I am writing to you on behalf of my drama class, which is participating in the Roundabout Theatre's Page to Stage Program this semester. We recently saw "Twentieth Century," and we wanted to thank you for taking the time after the performance to talk with us.

As part of our class, our teacher, Mr. Lord, recently gave us an exam on theatre "luminaries" who have played important roles in the history of the theatre. Our class, unfortunately, performed rather dismally on the test. Our teacher tried to make us, as theatre students, understand the importance of knowing about these individuals. He claimed, rather harshly, that if he pulled in ten strangers off the street they probably would have done better on the exam than we did. He claimed that anyone working in theatre would be familiar with the history of the individuals on his list.

I suggested we put his words to the test and, as we enjoyed seeing you recently, selected you to help us out.

Enclosed is a copy of the test. We would be very grateful if you could please take the test (at least parts I and II), completely unassisted, and using only your own knowledge of theatre history, and return the results to us. The outcome of your exam may sway our teacher to be more lenient on our grades.

We realize you may be very busy due to your schedule, but we would greatly appreciate it if you would take a small amount of time to complete the test. Thank you for your time.

Sincerely,

Tommy Thorsen and Classmates
Robert F. Kennedy High School
75-40 Parsons Blvd.
Flushing, New York 11366

Class letter to Alec Baldwin

Robert F. Kennedy High School
English/Drama
Mr. Lord

Name: _____Alec Baldwin___ Date: ___5.10.04___

I. Matching – Match the theatre luminary in Column I with the description in Column II by placing the corresponding letter to the left of the number. (30 points)

Column I		Column II
E	1. Agnes DeMille	a) Partner of F. Loewe
D	2. George Abbott	b) Acting teacher
G	3. Lorraine Hansberry	c) Director/Choreographer of **Best Little Whorehouse in Texas**
J	4. Neil Simon	d) Writer/Director; lived over 100 years
F	5. George C. Wolfe	e) Choreographer of **Oklahoma!**
B	6. Stanislavski	f) Runs the Public Theatre
C	7. Tommy Tune	g) Wrote **A Raisin in the Sun**
A	8. Alan Jay Lerner	h) Costume designer, **My Fair Lady**
H	9. Cecil Beaton	i) Choreographed **Cabaret, Chicago**
I	10. Bob Fosse	j) Author of **The Odd Couple**

II. Identification - From the list of names below, select the theatre luminary who correctly completes each sentence. (30 points)

Al Hirschfeld   Gower Champion
Michael Bennett   Helen Hayes
Ethel Merman   Tennessee Williams
David Merrick   Arthur Miller
Irving Berlin   Andrew Lloyd Webber

1. The man known as the Line King, _Al Hirschfeld_ was a caricaturist who captured the history of Broadway in his drawings.
2. Often referred to as "the first lady of the American theatre," _Helen Hayes_ had a Broadway theatre named after her.
3. A playwright, _Arthur Miller_ is best known as the author of **Death of a Salesman.**
4. On opening night of **42nd Street**, the director/choreographer _Gower Champion_, died.
5. The star of **Annie Get Your Gun** and **Gypsy**, _Ethel Merman_, is often called "the first lady of the musical theatre."

Alec Baldwin scored 100% on my English/Drama class exam.

A note from Alec.

He returned the exam, along with a note, "Dear Class! Thanks for your letter. **Alec Baldwin**," and a separate card for me: "Dear Mr. Lord, let me know how I did. Thanks for your letter. **Alec Baldwin**."

I thought it best to open the letter in full view of the class, lest they think I in some way might have altered Mr. Baldwin's responses. In front of the students, I reviewed the answers.

Perfect score!

I was feeling fully satisfied to have so successfully proven my point. The feeling lasted mere seconds.

"He must have cheated!" someone opined. Others quickly agreed.

Yes, you win some, you lose some!

(I have to think that, deep down, they believed Mr. Baldwin knew the answers but just didn't want to give me the satisfaction!)

Over the years, I have heard from so many former students (thanks, in large part, to Facebook), who seem to enjoy sharing their theatrical experiences with me . . . maybe almost as much as I like hearing about them.

Chapter Twenty-Six

THE POWERS OF THEATER

*S*ince I was a kid, I've always been shy. People who have gotten to know me in more recent years sometimes find this difficult to believe as I've managed to overcome many of my earlier inhibitions. It has been a gradual process, and I would still not exactly call myself an extrovert. But I have certainly come a long way in this regard, and to a great extent, I have theater to thank.

In fact, I have often touted theater as potentially transformative, sometimes in the most unusual ways.

Many years ago, while teaching at August Martin High School, I put together a student production that we called *Stay Tuned*. I hadn't thought about it much lately, but the recent live broadcast of newly-cast versions of old episodes of *All In the Family* and *The Jeffersons* put me freshly in mind of it. The broadcast was very much reminiscent of what we had done. At the time, *The Jeffersons*, about the title family who "moved on up to the East

Side" of Manhattan, was a top-rated sitcom, as were *Alice*, which starred **Linda Lavin** (many years before our encounter) as a waitress at a diner, and *Diff'rent Strokes*, which focused on a rich white man who adopts two young black boys.

Long before VCRs came into existence, I made audio tape recordings of the three shows and transcribed one episode of each, word for word, and, with my students playing all the popular characters, flung it across the stage of our auditorium.

I bring this up because of the young man who played George Jefferson. Seated in my class, he was as inconspicuous as could be. On stage, he was a different person! Following one performance, a colleague came up to me and asked if the actor on stage was really the same student she had come to know as **Jean Saintil**. She was incredulous, claiming that all the time he was in her class she had never once even heard his voice. I assured her it was, indeed, the same student!

Ah, yes, the powers of theater!

And there was the time we were involved in a theater workshop being run by a teaching artist from an enrichment program with which our school had been involved. As part of an exercise, the student participants were once asked to share emotional moments from their past. One member of the class, a football player who happened to be placed in the class in error and who I was able to persuade to remain, became so emotional that, in embarrassment, he rushed up the aisle and out the door of the auditorium.

Ordinarily, an event such as this could have led to merciless ridiculing by peers, but because of his status as an athlete, the young man emerged unscathed. In fact, because of who he was, he inadvertently transformed the entire class, as, one by one, each student opened up in front of the rest in ways I never witnessed before or since. The effects of that one period in the auditorium carried through for the rest of the semester. It was probably the greatest drama class I've ever taught!

Ah, yes, the powers of theater!

Theater has a way of reaching people—especially the young—unlike anything else I can think of. That is why I so frequently had to stand up to students' parents (and, in fact, colleagues, as well) who were constantly threatening to remove their child from a play production unless his or her grades or behavior in class improved. Luckily, I was usually able to dissuade them from such drastic measures.

I know first-hand what theater can do for a person. My shyness has always threatened to derail my "career" as an actor, but, to my own amazement, I've never let it get the best of me. My love for the stage outweighed my fears.

I sometimes still have to marvel at the many wonderful roles I've had the chance to play. These include Hysterium and Senex, in two different productions of *A Funny Thing Happened On the Way to the Forum*, Horace Vandergelder in *Hello, Dolly!*, Oscar Madison in *The Odd Couple* and Manolo Costazuela in the female version of that play, Wilbur Turnblad in *Hairspray*, Colonels Pickering and Buffalo Bill in *My Fair Lady* and *Annie Get Your Gun*, respectively, Herr Schultz in *Cabaret*, Hines in *The Pajama Game*, Mayor Shinn in *The Music Man*, Uncle Max in *The Sound of Music*, Mr. Baker in *Come Blow Your Horn*, Will Parker in *Oklahoma!*, Harry MacAfee in *Bye Bye Birdie*, Buddy Plummer in *Follies*, Nathan Detroit in *Guys and Dolls*, Buzz Richards in

Applause, Shem in *Two By Two,* Morris in *Fiorello!* and Jimmy Smith in *No, No, Nanette.*

You will undoubtedly note that as of now I have yet to play my dream role, The King in you-know-what. But it's not for lack of trying. I've auditioned five or six times at as many different theaters, and I've come close almost every time . . . but not quite close enough.

My only full-fledged leading man role (at least to this point) has been Jeff Moss, in *Bells Are Ringing,* directed by my old buddy **Larry Bloom**, in which I got to sing almost a dozen songs. I even took singing lessons to help me prepare, and, I must admit, I got quite a few compliments from friends who had been used to seeing me in the character roles that became my specialty.

One night, after a performance of the show, an older woman came up to congratulate me and mentioned that she had been in a production of *Bells Are Ringing,* too. I thought, "Oh, how sweet." I asked her, "Where did you do the show?" To this she replied completely matter-of-factly, "On Broadway." That stopped me in my tracks. "On Broadway?" I asked incredulously. "Yes," she confirmed. "You mean with **Judy Holliday**?" "Yes," she said. I asked her how she happened to come to see our show and she explained, simply enough, that she lived in the neighborhood.

I told her I was a reporter for the *Queens Chronicle* and that I would love to do a story about her, to which she agreed. That was the start of a friendship that exists to this day.

I should mention the woman's name: **Norma Doggett**, and her Broadway credits include not only *Bells Are Ringing,* but such shows as *Call Me Madam* and *Miss Liberty.* She is perhaps most proud of her role as one of the seven brides in the classic motion picture musical, *Seven Brides for Seven Brothers*, in which she appeared alongside **Jane Powell** and **Howard Keel**.

And I am most proud to call her a good friend.

Ah, yes, the powers of theater!

Meeting Norma Doggett after my performance in a local production of Bells Are Ringing. *We are still friends today.*

Chapter Twenty-Seven

REVIVED OR REVISED?

*I*t seems that with increasing frequency when a show is being re-mounted, the new production team deems it necessary to make changes of one sort or another in order to make the piece more acceptable to today's audiences. It might involve tweaking the original ending (witness the debate over the most recent rendering of *My Fair Lady*) or, perhaps, slight alterations in lyrics of well-known songs (*Kiss Me, Kate* comes easily to mind). In extreme cases (the latest revival of *Oklahoma!* is a controversial example), a classic might undergo a drastic re-thinking, sometimes without a single word being changed.

Along these lines, I recently asked the question, "Should plays be revised to be more politically correct?" The responses were overwhelmingly one-sided.

My take was as follows: "I think not. Most plays that are given revivals are classics for a reason: They were good—or even great. Leave them alone, I say. People should understand that they are products of their times. To alter them is disrespectful to the plays and their creators. And, for the most part, such 'updates' end up ruining the plays."

Some friends replied shortly but sweetly:

Mike Gannon, one of my editors at the *Queens Chronicle*, and an avid theater fan: "No. Next question."

Helen Elaine, whom I met through Broadway Blockbusters, one of the premier local production companies, run by **Andrew J. Koslosky,** one of my oldest theater acquaintances: "No, leave them alone."

Meredith Hoddeson, a Facebook friend and fellow collector of theatrical memorabilia: "Could not agree more! Keep classics as they were."

Alice Goldman Kasten: "Definitely not. They reflect the times in which they were written."

Bill Logan: "I agree. The one exception (to me) is the revisal of *Cabaret*. It became what it wanted to but couldn't" (when it opened in 1966).

Kathleen Hassett Hochberg: "And how could we ever know how far we've come?"

Guy DeMatties agreed: "No! They are products of their time . . . the same as books. How are future generations going to actually LEARN from the wrongs of generations past?"

A couple of friends got into a discussion about a recent rendering of a **Lerner & Loewe** classic:

Ron Spivak: "I completely agree. If you can't do *My Fair Lady* with the ending as written, do another show. Or write a new one!"

Melanie Lee: *"My Fair Lady* itself changed the ending of *Pygmalion."*

Ron Spivak: "Yes, but *My Fair Lady* wasn't trying to be *Pygmalion."*

Others got into a friendly debate over a controversial production of *Our Town*:

Larry Bloom: "I am in total agreement with you, Mark. A few years ago, I travelled to the Barrow Street Theatre to see an updated version of *Our Town* by **Thornton Wilder**, directed by **David Cromer**. I was concerned that the script would be altered but I am happy to report that wasn't the case. Subtle changes were made to the blocking that made the show more current and relevant. When the 'stage manager' . . . sat among the audience, I appreciated it—we were all involved in the play!"

Miles Tepper: "Give me the original any time. Remember when the stage manager took out his cell phone? Come on!"

Larry Bloom: "It was a bold move!"

Miles Tepper: "Bold, maybe, but bad. It was a slice of life rooted in time and place. A masterpiece that never should have been tampered with."

Larry Bloom: "I respectfully disagree!"

And then there was the *Carousel* discussion:

Marilyn Garfinkel: "I have mixed feelings about this. I really love the music in *Carousel,* but the abuse done by Billy Bigelow is hard to watch, especially when he is constantly forgiven for even his worst transgressions. How he made it to heaven is beyond me. I don't believe in 'intentions.' I believe a person should be judged by his or her actions. The scene where Billy comes back to earth and slaps his daughter and, when she discusses it with her mother, Julie says, 'It is possible, dear, for someone to hit you, hit you hard, and not hurt at all,' makes me wince. I do understand that's how it was written, but I feel really uncomfortable hearing those words. So, although I love the music, I do not watch this show any longer."

Kevin Craig: "This is a prime example of a show that might not have aged well yet still encapsulates how gender roles and societal expectations have evolved. Billy Bigelow doesn't deserve forgiveness and he does suffer for his mistakes but it's more about Julie's growth as a character that can have modern implications of independence and strength despite abusive circumstances. I would love it if our society no longer had domestic violence as a daily scar on humanity's progression but since it still exists, the final message of the musical could wind up being helpful to survivors of abuse; therefore, there's still relevance within the outdated and somewhat uncomfortable plot."

And another discussion surrounding the longest-running musical in American history:

Virginia Blackert: "No, No, No, Noooooo! Theater is historical! Don't erase history to save anyone's precious 'feelings.' I saw a rendition of *The Fantasticks* with the rape number re-written. Ridiculous. I had never walked out on a show—but I did that night."

Mitchell Kessler: "Yes, it was actually done at the official production while it ran at Snapple Theater. While I regretted the change, I accepted it. Rape is a serious matter and I could see people being offended."

Virginia Blackert: "It was a mistake and a stupid thing to do. If I took my teen to see a show that included 'rape' or the word 'nigger,' there would be far more for us to discuss than if some clown decided to whitewash the show. As far as I'm concerned, the only 'official' production was the show as written and performed at Sullivan Street."

Kevin Craig: "When tackling 'El Gallo' in *The Fantasticks* about five years ago, the 'alternate lyrics' were provided but the choice was up to our production team if we wanted to stick to the original, potentially offensive version or go with the cleaner take. Though sensitive to the topic, we decided to go with the original lyrics and were prepared to face audience reprisals but there weren't any."

Andrew Dinan: "For whom are we making the changes? Let's look at the Rape Ballet. Are you omitting or amending because you and your peers view it as an example of toxic masculinity or do you sense that in today's climate, knowing your audience, that it will build a barrier between them and their enjoyment of the show? The former I would have issues with, the latter not."

Others offered an assortment of astute observations:

Myles Moffit, one of the great dramatic actresses on our local stages: "I have seen several different (productions of) *Julius Caesar* in my lifetime and many clearly reflected the political environment."

Mitchell Kessler: "Generally, modernizing language in an old piece ruins its authenticity. Mankind needn't become humankind in an old play. The PC word didn't exist then, and people would notice and groan. The original use of the N-word in 'Ol' Man River' from *Show Boat* was later softened . . . I would still be jarred by the N-word."

Jeffrey Tierney, a triple threat I very much enjoyed directing in a production of *Gypsy*: "That question sort of arose during *Kiss Me, Kate*. It's not the best in terms of promoting women's equality since it's based off *The Taming of the Shrew*, but it reminds us of how things once (hopefully) were. Shows are meant to teach us."

Vincent Schicchi, a professional make-up artist with whom I once appeared on stage in an original vampire play: "No! Absolutely not. Would we rewrite *The Grapes of Wrath* to not have the 'breast feed' scene? Would we re-name you-know-who from *Tom Sawyer?* No . . . We can be more empathetic to causes now if we choose, but to re-write history to please people is . . . well . . . show me much of a difference between that and burning books."

Cesar F. Sostre: "Nooooooo! Political correctness is one of the things wrong with our society and I highly suspect it puts a real damper on creativity."

Miles Tepper: "No! Besides being tantamount to 'artistic theft' of the original, I am hard pressed to even think of a single 'updated revision' that even came close to the artistic worth of the original."

Chapter Twenty-Eight

SOME BASICS OF THEATER ETIQUETTE

*O*ver the years, I've taken dozens of classes on trips to the theater—to Broadway as well as to local productions. I even had the opportunity to bring a class to see one of my own performances . . . playing Pop in the Queens College production of *The Pajama Game*, a show in which I had played Hines years earlier.

This came about quite unexpectedly. I got a telephone call in school one day from a professor at the college, inviting me to bring a class to see a production of *Guys and Dolls*. Naturally, I leapt at the opportunity. The circumstances were perfect. Not only was the show a classic that everyone should experience, but tickets were very cheap, the college was within walking distance of our school, and I was more than proud to take my students on a visit to my alma mater.

The professor on the other end of the phone conversation turned out to be none other than **Charles Repole**, a veteran performer/director who was now wearing yet another hat. I was delighted to meet him and shared with him my admiration for his performance on Broadway in *Very Good Eddie*, for which he had earned a Tony Award nomination many years prior.

We became friends and, inspired by Charlie, I signed up for one of his classes. Over the next few years, I took several more and, eventually, I was able to apply those classes toward a salary differential, earning me an increase in pay. For that, I am forever grateful to Charlie. But I digress—yet again!

One of his classes required that each student audition for the upcoming college musical. For years I had attended performances at the college, and I always wished I could have performed on that same stage. Was this my chance, at last? Well, things worked out and it was a wonderful experience in every way. I think my students enjoyed seeing me in a whole new light.

One of the things I've always been most proud of is getting complimented on my students' behavior from fellow audience members. My favorite comment of all was from a woman who came up to me as we were making our way up the aisle toward the exit after we had seen a performance on Broadway. The play escapes me after all these years, but I've never forgotten what that woman said.

Somehow she had been given a seat right in the midst of our group. She was surrounded by about 30 of my students and, much as I always tried to prepare them on how to behave at the theater, you never knew when someone might act inappropriately in some way. To be honest, the arrangement made me feel quite ill at ease. I shouldn't have worried.

As we were leaving, the woman noticed this rather young-looking crowd all around her. She turned to me and said, "Oh, I didn't even realize I was sitting with a school group." That made my day. The students hadn't heard her remark, but I couldn't wait to share it with them the next day in class. And all it took was a review of some of the basic rules of proper behavior.

One of my recent Facebook questions addressed this very issue: "What's one rule of theater etiquette you'd like people to follow?"

I offered this response: "Plain and simple: I wish people (in the audience) would not talk during a performance."

Here are some of the other reminders offered by various friends:

Marilyn Garfinkel: "I wish people would arrive on time."

Jennifer Cové, a recent Facebook friend addition who performs as a singer and actress: "I wish people would not blatantly take out their cell phones."

Therese Brand, whom I met many years ago while working on a production of *Two By Two*: "Saw *The Dinner Party* with **John Ritter** and **Henry Winkler**. Someone's cell went off. Ritter broke character, told them about themselves, and went right back into character. That was so cool!"

Barri Sperber Feuer: "Don't crinkle candy or snack wrapper during the performance."

Edward Santos: "I wish people could go without eating for the two-and-a-half hours. This is not a movie theater."

Judith Mermelstein: "Don't clap to the rhythm of the curtain call music! Applaud for the performers!"

For **Andrew Dinan**, singing along is a definite no-no: "Reminds me of a comic who once said, 'I didn't pay 50 bucks to hear **Crosby, Stills, Nash** and Stephanie Abramowitz.'"

Marilyn Garfinkel: "Don't kick the back of the seat in front of you. And please tell your children not to do this."

Alex L. Mermelstein, a former student of mine who comes from a family of performers: "I'd love to see more audience members get dressed up to see a show. People used to wear suits, tuxedos, all kinds of fancy dresses, and it was amazing . . . it looked awesome."

Louise Guinther: "I wish people would get up automatically at intermission and let other people out of their row. There seems to be an epidemic of people who want to sit in the theater throughout intermission, and I can't ever get out to stretch my legs without getting a dirty look from the sedentary crowd."

Barri Sperber Feuer: "Don't wear light-up shoes to the theater." Once, she recalled, "There was a constant strobe light of flashes in the row in front of me."

Jacqueline Schnapp Schwartz: "**Stephen Sondheim** said it all in 'Invocation and Instructions to the Audience.'"

[That number, incidentally, was originally written for *A Funny Thing Happened On the Way to the Forum*, but was ultimately used as the opening number of another Sondheim musical, *The Frogs*, and it is well worth a listen.]

Turning the attention from the audience to the actors, **Jef Lawrence** said: "I don't like actors to greet the audience after the show while still in costume. It's obviously fine in children's theater. But staying in costume breaks the fourth wall. I've seen this done on Broadway, too, and it isn't right."

Debbie Vogel offered some advice from a professional's perspective: ""f you're not feeling well, let the front-of-house staff know. Please don't say nothing if you messed up the rest room because you're embarrassed. There is a porter on staff to clean up the mess. It's very unpleasant for your fellow patrons to find it during intermission. We can get you assistance if you need medical attention. Most important, please, if there's an emergency, let a staff member know. The show must go on, but not at anyone's health or safety risk."

I'd like to add a few additional reminders, what I call my practical list of "don'ts" for every theatergoer.

Don't talk back to the actors. They can usually hear—if not always see—you. I found out first-hand about this. I attended a performance of the little-known musical, *Tricks*, based on a play by **Moliere**. It ran at the Alvin Theatre (now the Neil Simon) for a grand total of eight performances in early 1973. It was the only time I can recall sitting in a box seat on Broadway (for $11.00), and at times, the actors, including **Rene Auberjonois** and **Walter Bobbie**, seemed to be directly beneath us, so far did the box overhang the stage. At one point, it was Auberjonois' character, I believe, who, seated nearby but not wanting to get involved in whatever might have been happening on stage at the time, said something to the effect, "Don't ask me. I'm an innocent bysitter." I loved the pun and, without realizing it, I let out a rather loud laugh and repeated, "Innocent bysitter." Auberjonois, hearing me, looked up and gave an appreciative smile. I was quite embarrassed by it all!

Don't wear oversized hats or other head apparel that could block the view of people sitting behind you.

Don't let your cranky child ruin the experience for everyone else. If your child begins to cry, yell, squirm, twist or, in any other way, disturb, please take the tot out to the lobby.

Don't fidget in your seat or sway from side to side. Doing this makes those behind you do the same.

Don't leave before the show is over to beat the crowd out the door. Show the actors some appreciation by way of your applause at the curtain call.

Chapter Twenty-Nine

DO WE HAVE TIME FOR ONE MORE LIST?

*T*his one was all about songs: (a) Favorite title song (meaning a song that shares its title with the show it's from; and (b) Favorite comic number from a musical.

On the day I posed that question (these things have a way of changing from moment to moment), I went with (a) "Mame" and (b) "Everybody Ought to Have a Maid" from *A Funny Thing Happened On the Way to the Forum*.

What did some of my friends have to say on the matter?

Marilyn Garfinkel: (a) "Oklahoma!," (b) Tie: "Always Look On the Bright Side of Life" from *Spamalot* and "I Cain't Say No" from *Oklahoma!*

Debbie Vogel: (a) "Applause," (b) "Brush Up Your Shakespeare" from *Kiss Me, Kate*

Alex L. Mermelstein: (a) "Little Shop of Horrors," (b) "Springtime for Hitler" from *The Producers*

Andrew Dinan: (a) "On a Clear Day You Can See Forever," (b) "I Am the Very Model of a Modern Major General" from *The Pirates of Penzance*

Therese Brand: (a) "Mame," (b) "You Can't Get a Man with a Gun" from *Annie Get Your Gun*

John Baratta: (a) "Hello, Dolly!," (b) "Who's Got the Pain?" from *Damn Yankees*

Michael Brooks: (a) Tie: "Mame" and "The Sound of Music," (b) "Brush Up Your Shakespeare" from *Kiss Me, Kate*

Gary Eisele: (a) "Oklahoma!," (b) Tie: "Brush Up Your Shakespeare" from *Kiss Me, Kate* and "Two Ladies" from *Cabaret*

Adrian Strizhak, whom I met online while doing research for a play I was writing: (a) "Cabaret," (b) "Strong Woman Number" from *I'm Getting My Act Together and Taking It On the Road*

Bruce Levy: (a) "Hello, Dolly!," (b) "Comedy Tonight" from *A Funny Thing Happened On the Way to the Forum*

Judith Mermelstein: (a) "Anything Goes," (b) "Getting Married Today" from *Company*

Miles Tepper: (a) "Children of Eden," (b) "Comedy Tonight" from *A Funny Thing Happened On the Way to the Forum*

Alan Newmark: (a) "Camelot," (b) "I Hate Men" from *Kiss Me, Kate*

Lloyd Baum: (a) 'Milk and Honey," (b) "The Song That Goes Like This" from *Spamalot*

Jef Lawrence: (a) "Man of La Mancha," (b) "Brush Up Your Shakespeare" from *Kiss Me, Kate*

Larry Bloom: (a) "The Sound of Music," (b) "Everybody Ought to Have a Maid" from *A Funny Thing Happened On the Way to the Forum*

Chapter Thirty

AS A TEACHER I'VE BEEN LEARNING...

*B*eing involved in theater for so long has taught me many things . . . about how to be better at it and also about life in general. As a teacher, I have always believed in the importance of introducing theater into my students' lives and I've tried to help them develop an appreciation for it.

I was wondering what my friends—those who are involved in productions and those who enjoy seeing them—have gotten out of the experience.

So, I asked . . .

"What is one thing you've learned from theater?" I suggested that their answers could be based on a lesson taught by a particular show or from the process of doing theater in general . . . or both.

From theater, I said, "I've learned that practice does, indeed, make perfect . . . that there's no substitute for rehearsal . . . no shortcuts that work as well."

Marilyn Garfinkel: "I grew up in a home where my dad and sister were both active in community theater and my other sister and my mom loved it. Broadway music was often on the stereo or my father was playing it on the piano. I was introduced to it all at a very young age. I am glad that my horizons were expanded by growing up with good exposure to theater. I learned that starting so young to appreciate theater made me a lifelong fan. I have done the same with my kids, with similar results."

To this comment, I responded, "I think most of us who love theater were introduced at a young age. I wonder . . . do you think it's possible to become hooked later in life?"

Marilyn replied, "I think anything is possible. But the earlier the better. Most of my 'rock and roll' friends, who I met in high school, have absolutely no interest in theater."

James Gillespie, one of the backbones at a local community group, Maggie's Little Theater: "It is possible to get involved later in life! I only started on-stage six years ago. My daughter encouraged me to audition for *Fiddler on the Roof.* They needed men with beards. I had a blast and made new friends. Next thing I know . . . What have I learned? So many things. I learned to let loose every once in a while. I learned that there are many facets to theater and being on stage is only one of them."

Alison Feuer Pascuzzi: "I learned to frantically change costumes in a closet with another person who's doing the same. I learned that Sardi's is to Broadway as 'the diner' is to community theater. I feel that learning to wait for cues and to ad lib when needed are excellent preparation for motherhood."

Larry Bloom: "The lesson that I've learned from theater is that every person has something to contribute to the success of a production. It doesn't matter how big or small a person's role is. Their contribution should always be acknowledged and appreciated."

Jef Lawrence: "I learned the world needs music. Whether it's a musical, a play or abstract performance, music is a necessary component."

Debbie Vogel: "I've learned so much about the painful lives many playwrights had and how they turned that distress into art that has helped other human beings. A perfect example is **O'Neill**'s *Long Day's Journey Into Night*. I saw it in elementary school and it helped me empathize and understand other people's problems. Also, after open heart surgery, I refused to take morphine and used more natural remedies to get rid of the pain. I didn't want to go through what Mary Tyrone did. Plays do influence our daily lives."

Miles Tepper: "I learned that to be successful as an actor on stage, you have to find a way to combine two antithetical elements: You have to be both 'natural' and 'larger than life' simultaneously. If you do one without the other, you are likely to be disappointed (and disappointing to the audience). If you are just 'natural,' it's likely you'll be boring. We are all 'natural' as we go through our day, but it's not likely anyone will be transfixed or even moved by what we do. If you are just 'larger than life,' you risk not being 'real.' The best British actors do it. They are not afraid to combine 'the method' with external action that comes across as, I guess, a heightened reality."

Judith Mermelstein: "From *Godspell* I learned stuff I didn't know about Jesus. From *1776* I learned stuff I didn't know about the writing of the Declaration of Independence. From scene-study class, I learned that the audience has to be shown (not told) what each character wants. From **Chekhov**, I learned not to put a gun onstage unless it's going to be fired before the end of the play. And from community theater, I learned how to clean a tuxedo with a Sharpie. I think my kids learned that they could be respected colleagues of people of all ages when they did community theater, a wonderful lesson in intergenerational perspective."

Candee Sheppard: "I learned to really listen to what is going on when I performed in *She Loves Me*. My partner-in-crime was very creative with his lines and I had to 'stay in the moment' to keep the flow of the scene sometimes. It was a fun experience, actually."

Jacqueline Schnapp Schwartz: "I had one of those partners in *Butterflies Are Free*. Extremely creative in his blocking. He claimed that as a method actor, a blind boy wouldn't know where he was going. LOL."

Michael Brooks: "I learned that the Boy Scout motto, 'Be prepared,' which I learned in my very young days, applies very strongly to the theater."

Jacqueline Schnapp Schwartz: "During a blizzard, we had more people on stage than in the audience. The director told us that the audience deserved the best show possible because they made the difficult journey to see us. The message: Always give your best."

Loria Parker: "I've learned that my years in the theater prepared me for many roles I've played in 'real life': caregiver, travel agent, waitress (of course!), and my favorite, wife to the best husband in the world."

Melanie Lee: "The show-within-a-show, 'The Small House of Uncle Thomas,' in *The King and I* shows the importance of theater. Tuptim read the novel, *Uncle Tom's Cabin*, identified with it, and presented it as a ballet with narration and song. While most of the audience enjoyed the spectacle, Anna got the real message and so did King Mongut. He wasn't happy. Theater can raise our emotions with its spectacle and deepen our understanding with its ideas."

Oren Sachs, one of the few guys on the local scene who feels comfortable dancing on stage: "I have learned to love the process and the people even when they can be frustrating, which is why after the completion of every show I have felt both relief and depression."

Chapter Thirty-One

GETTING TO KNOW YOU

early two decades had passed since I last saw "Mrs. Anna" after the performance that evening in the park near Lincoln Center, so my hopes of meeting up with her every 10 years had long since evaporated. But thoughts of somehow making contact with her again kept crossing my mind every once in a while.

One night, in 1992, I was watching the Emmy Awards . . . the 44th annual primetime event. Though I was mostly interested in the comedy categories, one award—for Outstanding Supporting Actor in a Drama Series—made me leap to my feet with excitement, and it was for a show I had never even watched.

The winner was **Richard Dysart**, for his role in the long-running *L.A. Law*, a program that was set in a Los Angeles law firm, with cases that "ranged from the thought-provoking to the trivial, enabling the program to mix seriousness with humor," as described in *Total Television* by **Alex McNeil**.

Accepting his award, Dysart acknowledged his wife—by name. I was stunned and thought, "I found her!"

He was a well-established actor and likely would be fairly easy to track down. I figured I could contact him—maybe at the studio where the series was filmed—and, through him, get in touch with Cathy.

My anticipation was off the charts but, alas, short-lived. I looked up Dysart on the burgeoning World Wide Web for any leads it might offer. And that's when reality struck. Turns out he was married to an artist whose name was **Kathryn Jacobi**, not **Catherine Jacoby**.

It took me a while to get used to modern technology, but a few years later I felt ready to try to reactivate my search. I looked up Cathy on the Internet, to no avail. Every time I entered her name, information came up about a woman named **Loria Parker**. Who is that, I thought, and why does she keep popping up? It would take some time before I would figure out the connection—a long time!

Fast forward another dozen years or so, to 2010. I picked up a copy of *The New York Times* and came upon an obituary for one **Coleman Jacoby**, a man whose name I immediately recognized. He had been an Emmy Award-winning comedy writer during television's golden age, having contributed material for **Sid Caesar** and **Imogene Coca** on the immensely popular *Your Show of Shows*, as well as for **Jackie Gleason, Phil Silvers** and other top name entertainers of the period.

I knew of Jacoby from Cathy's bio in *The King and I*, which read in part: "The daughter of singer **Violeta Velero Hall** and television writer **Coleman Jacoby**, Catherine is a graduate of the High School of Performing Arts in New York City."

Tucked in the middle of the obit was a line about Jacoby's survivors, among them his daughter Catherine of Mineola, Long Island.

"She's right here in New York," I thought to myself. And I had actually passed Mineola on many occasions traveling on the Long Island Expressway on my way to direct shows for the Patio Players. My search had just gotten a whole lot easier.

Shortly thereafter, I decided to try my luck on social media . . . this time on Facebook. Again, the name **Loria Parker** surfaced and I began to suspect that Catherine had perhaps changed her name.

I sent the following personal message to Loria:

"Hi, Loria! My name is Mark. I'm not sure you're the person I'm looking for, but I hope you are. By any chance, did you play Anna in *The King and I* at the Tapia Theatre in Puerto Rico in 1963? If so, I wanted to tell you that that production changed my life. Please let me hear back from you."

I got this response:

"Wow! Yes, that's me. I can't believe you remember or anyone remembers, but I remember doing the show I think with **Raul Davila**. I hope it changed your life for the good. Please let me know. Best, Cathy."

Let her know? Here was my invitation to continue our dialogue. So, I laid it all out, relating the story that I shared earlier in these pages:

"Oh, I am so glad to hear from you and to see that it is YOU. Of course, I'm talking about how the show changed my life for the good! I can't begin to tell you the effect that show had on me. I was nine years old at the time and my parents took my brother and me to see it. It was the first theater I had ever experienced, and that night, my life changed forever. I don't know if it was that particular show or the performances by you and **Raul Davila**, or just being at a very impressionable age, or what. But it struck a chord in me that I sometimes find incredible myself. Strangely enough, I mostly identified with Anna (as I had even at that age already known that I wanted to become a teacher). I think I was so impressed with the influence she had on The King and his country. I could tell you details that I remember about that production that would probably amaze you . . . Theater has been a major part of my life ever since . . . not professionally, but in community theater. And, of course, *The King and I* remains my favorite show to this day. The part of The King is one I've wanted to play my whole life, but despite half a dozen auditions, never landed it. I know I'm not the right 'type,' but it's a role I feel to my very core. My family eventually moved back to New York. About 10 years after that production at the Tapia, I saw an account in a newspaper that *The King and I* was going to be done in the park by Lincoln Center. Naturally, I was planning to see it. And then I saw that some of the performers from the Tapia were going to be in it, including yourself and **Raul Davila**. I waited to try to meet you both after the show . . . 'The King' apparently slipped away unnoticed, but I did get to meet you. I even had you sign my program from the Tapia Theatre. I remember you were shocked that anyone would still have that program. You signed it, 'Best wishes for the next 10 years.' I was truly sorry to learn of the passing of **Raul Davila** several years ago, especially since I

never had the chance to meet him to share with him my senti-
ments. And I do want to offer you my condolences on the
recent loss of your father. It was actually through his obituary
in *The New York Times* that I was able to locate you under your
new name. Anyway, I thank you for responding to my original
correspondence and hope we can remain in touch. Perhaps
someday we could meet to share further memories, if you're so
inclined. I will also request you as a friend on Facebook, which
I hope you'll accept. Sincerely, Mark."

Well, Cathy accepted my friendship request almost immediately,
but there was no response to my rather lengthy message. "She
probably needs time to write back an equally lengthy response,"
I thought to myself. Days passed. Could it be that somehow she
saw my friend request but not my message? Should I write
again to be sure she received it? On the advice of a friend, who
suggested Cathy might think I was stalking her, I decided not to
reach out again.

Three months later, much to my amazement, Cathy responded
to one of my weekly theater questions—yes, the very same ones
that led to this book! And she mentioned that she would be
performing in Manhattan and suggested that that might be a
great opportunity for us to meet.

Miracle of miracles, after all those years, I was going to have a
second chance to meet up with "Mrs. Anna." I had to remind
myself that, though I would be thrilled to meet her, she might
not be as enthused. After all, to her, I was probably just a fan of a
show that she had been in nearly 50 years earlier.

On my way to the show, I picked up a single rose for her, a token
of my appreciation for what she and the show had come to

mean to me. I stepped up to the box office (actually, a table placed just beyond the entranceway to the restaurant where the show was to take place).

There was a lovely older woman behind the table who asked me my name and if I knew anyone in the show?" "My name is **Mark Lord**," I said.""I came to see **Loria Parker**."

She checked my name off on the reservations list and, looking up, said,""Oh, there she is, right behind you."

This is the moment . . . the one I'd been waiting for for years. I turned around and we found ourselves face to face. Cathy (to me, that's who she'll always be) and I greeted each other with a warm hug such as the kind two long-separated friends would give. And she continued to hold on tightly to me for what seemed like a solid minute—if not longer.

I guess she was as glad to see me as I was her!

I gave her the rose. She introduced me to her husband, **Gerry Janssen**, and suggested I ask for a seat at his table, which I did. She wished us to enjoy the show and took off for backstage. Gerry and I made small talk (truth be told, Gerry was sometimes a man of few words, so I did what I could to keep the conversation going).

The show began and, for the first time since 1973, I got to hear Cathy sing . . .""If He Walked Into My Life" from *Mame* and'" Nobody Does It Like Me" from one of my favorite musicals, the all-but-forgotten *Seesaw*. She was wonderful, as expected. Dinner was wonderful. The entire evening was wonderful. At its conclusion, Cathy took me over to meet the show's producer, a robust, animated man named **Mark York**, who presented the show as a special event for The Ziegfeld Society, an organization he co-founded to honor the great showman **Florenz Ziegfeld** and preserve musical theater history through education and performance.

In introducing us, Cathy told Mark that I was the guy connected to *The King and I* and he immediately reacted in a way that suggested he was familiar with the whole story. I guess it meant as much to Cathy as it had to me.

And meeting Mark opened up a whole new chapter in my show business "career."

Chapter Thirty-Two

ZIEGFELD AND BEYOND

*C*athy (actually Loria, which is how most people who have made her acquaintance in more recent years know her) explained to **Mark York** that I was a writer and that I might be able to assist in editing a journal he published periodically for members of The Ziegfeld Society. It was called *The Ziegfeld Times*, and it featured stories about the organization, people associated with it, and other related topics. I would be glad to help, I told him, and also ended up contributing several articles, including one on Loria and another on **Michele McConnell**, who spent years playing Carlotta in Broadway's *The Phantom of the Opera*.

I was beginning to get a feel for life in the professional theater, which I enjoyed tremendously. Not long after, I mentioned to Mark that I would be interested in helping out backstage, if he could use my help. As it turned out, he could.

Over the next few years, I would stage manage a couple dozen of his shows. One of the earliest ones I worked on was *America's*

Funny Girl **Fanny Brice**, starring Loria in the title role. Who could ever have imagine "Mrs. Anna" and I would end up working on a show together?

Along the way, I have had the opportunity to work with an incredible array of talented performers—some top Broadway names, others up-and-comers—from whom I've learned a great deal . . . including the fact that when it comes to putting on a show, no matter where or on what level it might be, the preparation is the same. Remembering lines and lyrics is rarely, if ever, easy for anyone. Like those of us who toil on local stages, big name performers with years and years of experience still get nervous before a show. And like those of us who perform for little or no financial remuneration, they have a tendency to make noise backstage while the show is going on. I consider myself fortunate to have had the opportunity to observe first-hand how the pros do what they do, a topic I had taken up so many years earlier with **Harold Prince**.

And now I must ask your indulgence as I engage in more than a bit of name dropping, admittedly bragging about some of the people I've had the privilege to work with. **Carol Lawrence**, perhaps best known as the original Maria in Broadway's *West Side Story*, was the headliner in a Ziegfeld Society production called *A Salute to Rockette History II*, an expanded version of an earlier show on the same theme. At the time, I was preparing a production of my own with the Patio Players on Long Island, a salute to television and, in particular, *The* **Ed Sullivan** *Show*, television's longest-running variety program, which ran from 1948 until 1971. It was an original musical called *Our Really Big Shew*, an homage to Sullivan's pronunciation of the word "show," at least as many of those who did impressions of him would have it. I had to do a great deal of research while writing the show, which could be a drudgery, but working with Miss Lawrence gave me the opportunity to speak with a performer who had actually appeared on Sullivan's show, providing firsthand insight.

As she explained, each Sunday night, Sullivan's show went on the air live—a rarity nowadays but fairly common back then. Rehearsals, she explained, took place from early in the morning and lasted throughout the day until air time. Sullivan would typically arrive just in time for the final dress run-through. He was apparently a tough task master, and, if he didn't like a particular act, he would have no qualms about having it removed from the show and replaced by one of the acts he always had standing by. And week after week, year after year, the show went off with nary a hitch, except for Ed's frequent botching of his introductions, some of which have become legendary. Amazing how the show was able to keep up such a schedule for an incredible 23 seasons.

I also remember the professionalism of **The Rockettes**, who appeared in the Ziegfeld show. As I recall, they had all long since retired from the kick line, but you'd never know it from the discipline they displayed both on- and off-stage. When I cued them for their entrance, within a split second, they were all perfectly lined up backstage, and, without a second thought, automatically shifted into their famous Rockette stance.

Another great experience was working with **Sarah Rice**, the original Joanna in Broadway's *Sweeney Todd*, who was starring in *Folies-Bergere*, a tribute to Ziegfeld's inspiration for his Ziegfeld Follies. Nearly four decades after *Sweeney*, her voice remains a thing of true beauty, and to hear her sing live and in person is a wonder.

Lee Roy Reams, a familiar face along the Great White Way from his countless performances, is not only talented but a man of great wit. He's been in the business a long time and he has stories about everyone—which he is more than happy to share. Waiting backstage before going on, he would regale us with tales of his life upon the wicked stage—and hilarity would always ensue.

In *Ziegfeld's Cavalcade of Stars*, I was privileged to work with both **Carole Demas**, the original Sandy in Broadway's *Grease*, and **Anita Gillette**, who has had a long career on stage and screen, and who first delighted me when, as a kid, I heard her sing "The Secret Service" on the original cast recording of **Irving Berlin**'s final Broadway musical, *Mr. President.*

Another favorite of mine is **Jim Dale**, a Tony Award winner for his title role performance in *Barnum*, which I got to see during its long Broadway run. I've worked on a couple of shows with him, including a celebration of songwriter **Meredith Willson**, famous for *The Music Man* and *The Unsinkable Molly Brown*, among other shows, and in a tribute to the Ziegfeld Society as a celebration for its tenth anniversary season. And when I went to see him in his one-man off-Broadway show, *Just Jim Dale*, I was treated to a backstage tour courtesy of **Mark York**, Jim's long-time pianist.

Also a delight to work with was **Karen Ziemba**, another Tony Award winner with a great many credits to her name. At one point in one of the shows, someone needed to rest their microphone on the top of the piano, but it kept sliding off. We needed something that would not only keep it in place but would also look good, in keeping with Ziegfeld's (and **Mark York's**) penchant for glitz and glamour. Karen took out her large make-up case (actually, it was made of cloth, as I recall), dumped the contents on a table backstage, and suggested that would offer the perfect solution. It did. Here's a star who is as down to earth as she is talented.

A very special memory came from working with **Liliane Montevecchi**, the acclaimed French singer and dancer who won a Tony Award for her performance in *Nine*, which I never got to see, and a nomination for *Grand Hotel*, which I did. Already in her early 80s when I first met her, she was a study in contrasts. When rehearsing, if she forgot a lyric, she would cuss like a sailor, but with her delightful accent, it only endeared her even more to everyone. While waiting to go on, she would seem so fragile, so delicate, so in need of being taken care of. Once, she asked me if I could get her a cup of coffee. There was none at the theater, so I made a quick run and was back within minutes. I apologized for bringing her coffee from a fast-food establishment, the closest place I could find. She offered to pay me for it, but I told her the pleasure was mine. I was glad—and relieved—when she told me the coffee was actually quite good!

The next time we did a show together, perhaps a year or two later, I reminded her of the incident. It apparently didn't make as big an impression on her as it had on me, as she seemingly had no recollection of it at all!

She would sit quietly by herself, fully looking her age. Then her name would be announced and she would spring to life, making a true star entrance, always to an enthusiastic welcome from the crowd, and wowing them with her singing, dancing, and the inevitable flashing of her never-ending legs.

You can probably imagine the sadness I felt when I learned of her passing not long after, but I am so glad that I had the chance to get to know her—even if for a few fleeting moments.

And then there is **Walter Willison**, a true Renaissance man: actor, singer, writer, director, producer. It was his rendition of "I Do Not Know a Day I Did Not Love You," on the original Broadway cast recording of *Two By Two*, to which I often sang along as a teenager already hooked on show tunes. It was a performance that earned Walter a Tony nomination as Best Featured Actor in a Musical, as well as a Theatre World Award in his Broadway musical debut.

He has also starred in, written and/or directed many of the Ziegfeld shows I worked on. I guess he was impressed with my work because he has since invited me to serve as stage manager on several shows he has directed on other stages. Watching him in action is always a learning experience for me and something I always look forward to.

I must also acknowledge another show business veteran from whom I have learned a lot. **Richard Skipper** has been involved in virtually every aspect of performing one could imagine, as an entertainer, emcee, raconteur, interviewer, writer, promoter, theater historian, arts advocate . . . you name it, he's probably done it!

I introduced myself to him one evening a few years ago following the Theatre World awards ceremony. I told him I knew of his work and would be interested in working with him. He seemed receptive enough and we exchanged the usual information; he said he would be in touch if he ever needed my assistance. True to his word, a few days later he called me, inviting me to stage manage his long-running *Richard Skipper Celebrates* series, a monthly talk/variety show held at the Laurie Beechman Theatre, at the corner of 42nd Street and Ninth Avenue in Manhattan. The shows feature top artists in the entertainment field, primarily known for their involvement in the cabaret scene, a whole new world for me. The shows were put together even more quickly than the Sullivan shows, a couple of hours before show time. Each show usually features three or four guest stars, who would each have 15 minutes to run through their numbers with the band. And then they were on. Just like that. We in community theater take just a bit longer!

Of course, these are pros. And, again, from watching them prepare and seeing them perform, I've learned a great deal. How could I not when we're talking about the likes of **Sarah Rice** (happily, our paths have crossed several times), **Sharon McNight, David Sabella, Sue Matsuki, Linda Purl, Lillias White, Jana Robbins, Diane J. Findlay, KT Sullivan, Christine Pedi**, and the original Dainty June herself, **Lane Bradbury**, all accomplished artists.

For this English teacher from Brooklyn, who grew up in Puerto Rico, was smitten by the smell of greasepaint at the age of nine, and who has had a great time these past 30-plus years performing in community theater, working with people like these and many others has been a remarkable experience . . . one for which I will always be grateful.

Chapter Thirty-Three

APPLAUSE, APPLAUSE

*B*efore we bring the curtain down on this enterprise, I thought for the curious among you I would end where this whole thing began, with the very first theater question that I posed on Facebook on June 8, 2012: "With the Tonys coming up, now might be a good time to start a periodic theater-related question of the day. First up: What is the one moment in a show guaranteed to get a round of applause?"

The Tonys, I might mention, have been an annual highlight of my life since March 28, 1971, the night I saw the awards' special 25th anniversary edition on television, a salute that included all the previous Best Musical winners with numbers performed by many of the original stars. I recorded the event on my reel-to-reel tape recorder, the most modern technology available at the time, marking the beginning of a long tradition—I've preserved, in one format or another, every Tony Awards show since!

But I digress, most likely for one last time on these pages!

In retrospect, that first question was a rather unusual one, and I really can't remember what inspired it.

First, I answered the question myself: "My vote goes to the moment when Anna and The King start whirling around the stage in 'Shall We Dance?'"

Need I even mention that's a reference to *The King and I*?

You know, I've seen that show performed more times than I could possibly count, everywhere from church basements to Broadway with the once and ever king himself, **Yul Brynner**, and every single time, without fail, as The King hesitatingly extends his hand before finally placing it firmly on Anna's waist, commands her to "come," pulls her gently towards him, and sweeps her off her feet, the audience, totally exhilarated, has responded with a resounding ovation.

Here is how some of my friends responded to that initial question:

Alex L. Mermelstein: "The bottle dance in *Fiddler* always gets a round of applause. Mostly by the audience, but often by the rest of the cast so you can't hear the Velcro when they take the bottles off."

Velcro? You mean the dancers don't actually balance those bottles themselves? Well, it depends. I've heard from some who have performed the dance that the "bottles" are oftentimes made of plastic, to prevent breakage should they happen to drop. Sometimes dancers wear special hats with the bottles attached to prevent them from falling. And magnets have been known to be used to help keep the bottles in place.

But why resort to such deceitful tactics? It's much more exciting to take a little risk—as long as you get plenty of practice beforehand. Broadway legend has it that during the original production, pink slips for each of the dancers in the number were placed inside their respective bottles. If a bottle were to fall and break, the dancer would be fired right there on the spot. How's that for motivation?

And, when no tricks are used, at the end of the number, the dancers can lean forward to show that the bottles really can fall off—usually to that great applause Alex was talking about.

John O'Hare put it this way: "Any show, anywhere, any time anyone does a kick line, be it a feeble lift of a foot or the synchronized perfection of **The Rockettes**, there is an almost Pavlovian reaction among audiences to start clapping."

John might well have mentioned a certain word in *A Funny Thing Happened On the Way to the Forum*, in which he once directed me, that never fails to bring the house down, just prior to intermission. Yes, a single word that gets one of the biggest laughs in a show filled with hilarity . . . but no spoilers here!

I was introduced to the show in 1972, via the first Broadway revival which, as a gift to the people of New York City, gave a free Fourth of July performance. Never one to miss out on such an opportunity, I raced to the theater and was lucky to snare a ticket. Not only was the show free, but the cast, which included **Phil Silvers** and **Larry Blyden** in the roles originated 10 years earlier by **Zero Mostel** and **Jack Gilford**, respectively, served as ushers, greeting patrons as we entered.

I'm not usually one to laugh out loud in the theater, but this show had me doing so almost without a break. And then came that moment when that word was uttered by Silvers. I, along with the entire audience, simply roared. You'll have to see the show some time, somewhere, to see what I'm talking about. I suspect it works every time.

Charles Cooper, a colleague on *Phoenix* with whom I had been out of touch for decades, surprised me by responding: "When the P.A. comes on and they 'kindly' remind the audience to mute or turn off their damned cell phones." Not really part of the show, but very true!

Joe Dowd said: "When Emile appears out of the shadows, all scruffy, in the final scene of *South Pacific*, as the children are singing 'Dites Moi.' I even gasp at this, still, and I know it's coming."

Some responders simply found it too difficult to select just one such moment. **Barri Sperber Feuer** responded like this: "The very end of *Les Miserables* when Valjean dies and Fantine comes to take him to heaven and the whole cast starts singing 'When Tomorrow Comes' in unison—gets me every time. And, of course, that moment in *Wicked* when Elphaba flies at the climax of 'Defying Gravity.'"

And **Florence Ondré**, one of our local stellar leading ladies, with whom I once shared the stage in a production of *Mame*, referred to the role in which she received so much acclaim: "When Mame Dennis wins over the whole family on Beauregard's southern plantation after her rollicking ride which winds up with her actually catching the fox and everyone sings."

She couldn't let it go just at that, but turned to a second iconic **Jerry Herman** character: "And when Dolly Levi appears at the top of the stairs in that red gown and feathered headdress as the waiters whisper asides of 'she's here . . . she's back' right into the title song. What lovely moments when funny goes straight to the heart."

Getting straight to the heart: That's what theater is really about, isn't it?

EPILOGUE

*W*ell, I guess that's about it for now!

Never in my wildest imagination could I ever have anticipated where one simple little question would lead.

I have certainly enjoyed traveling back in time, re-reading the thousands of comments that my friends so generously shared with me and the world on Facebook. Doing so made me realize, as if I needed a reminder, just how wonderful the theater can be. In addition to everything else it does, theater managed to inspire a group of diversified people to offer wide-ranging opinions and to, ultimately, come together as one. I hope all of you have enjoyed taking this journey with me—both on my page and through this publication.

I appreciate each and every one of you—those who contributed to the creation of this book as well as all of you who now hold a copy of it in your hands.

I hope to continue with a Weekly Theater Question each Friday morning well into the future . . . and that this little forum of ours will grow and grow and have a long, open-ended run. I have no aspirations that it will break the *Phantom* longevity record, but let's see where things lead.

I look forward to hearing from friends both old and new with your thoughts, feelings and other reactions to this one tie that binds us to one another.

I can't imagine what my life would have been without theater in it; as far as I'm concerned, there is no substitute for it . . . nothing else quite like it on the face of the earth. I can't think of a single other thing that has theater's ability to touch our emotions, to change our perspective, to temporarily take us out of reality (or perhaps thrust us all the more deeply into it), to transform us. In my case—as it undoubtedly did for many of you—theater literally changed my life.

I hope each of you will continue to share your love of the theater. Please do what you can to inspire others to discover its magical powers.

To all of you and to the theater, my deepest gratitude.

APPENDIX - "THAT OLD FAMILIAR RING"

If you're like me—and if you're reading this, we likely have more than a little in common—you've probably found yourself uttering a line from a show tune that has unconsciously worked its way into your everyday vernacular. Sometimes it works in reverse; a particular phrase you've used all your life suddenly appears in a song—**Kander & Ebb** have been very good at including time-tested sayings in their compositions, like "The Apple Doesn't Fall" in *The Rink* and "The Grass Is Always Greener" in *Woman of the Year*—and, from then on, you're compelled to burst into song every time you hear someone utter it. I amazed myself as to just how many references to shows I (mostly) inadvertently made as I was putting this book together. For your enjoyment, I have listed on the following pages all such instances—at least those that I could pinpoint. I'd be willing to bet that you've uncovered at least a few others that I have overlooked. After all, I warned you to keep an eye out for them!

"Who am I, anyway?" is, of course, a question asked in "I Hope I Get It," in *A Chorus Line.*

'The subject I like most" appears in the introduction to "Getting to Know You," in *The King and I.*

"A Typical Day" is the title of the opening number from *Li'l Abner.*

Two On the Aisle is the title of a musical revue that starred **Bert Lahr** and **Dolores Gray** in the early 1950s.

"Days Gone By" is a song from *She Loves Me.*

"One singular moment" is a take-off on "one singular sensation," again from *A Chorus Line.*

"Nobody's Perfect" is the title of a hilarious duet from the two-character musical, *I Do! I Do!,* that starred **Mary Martin** and **Robert Preston**.

"As a teacher I've been learning" is another phrase from the introduction to "Getting to Know You."

"Getting to Know You" . . . well, by now, that is pretty clear!

"Applause, applause" is from the title song of the musical, *Applause,* based on the motion picture, *All About Eve.*

AND THEN WE COME TO THE BOOK'S INTRODUCTION, WHICH FEATURES SOME SAMPLES OF ITS OWN:

"Many moons ago" is reminiscent of a song from *Once Upon a Mattress,* an adaptation of *The Princess and the Pea.*

"Tradition." Sometimes a single word is all it takes . . . especially if it's the title of one of the greatest opening numbers ever written, from, needless to say (but I'll say it anyway), *Fiddler On the Roof.*

"An English teacher" was not only my profession but a song title from *Bye Bye Birdie.*

AS FOR THE ACTUAL TEXT, WOW! I SPOTTED MORE REFERENCES THAN EVEN I COULD HAVE IMAGINED!

"An old familiar ring" (chapter 1) reminded me of a song from that little-known musical, *Jimmy,* one of several, including *Fiorello!* and *Mayor,* that have been written about former mayors of New York City.

"I'll tell you . . . I don't know," (chapter 2) as spoken by Tevye in "Tradition," was the most apt way I could think of to explain my own bewilderment over my fascination with the theater.

"Let's start at the very beginning" (chapter 2) is, of course, the opening line of "Do Re Mi" from *The Sound of Music,* and a most appropriate way to begin a book, don't you think?

I had to slip in "happy hunting" (chapter 2) as a way of encouraging you to search for musical clues. It's the great title song from a show that starred **Ethel Merman**, in one of her lesser-known vehicles, though I think it has a wonderful score.

"As far as I'm concerned" (chapter 3) was the title of a song I sang in *Two By Two,* which caused me great embarrassment the night I performed a much-abbreviated version of it. (See Chapter 21.)

I refer to Puerto Rico as being what people used to think of as "an island floating in the middle of the world somewhere" (chapter 3), which called to mind a song in *Pacific Overtures.*

It's called "The Advantages of Floating In the Middle of the Sea."

"A most delightful way" (chapter 3) is a phrase that also appears in "Thank Heaven for Little Girls,' from the film and subsequent stage musical, *Gigi*.

"The time of his life" (chapter 4) is reminiscent of a song title in *Dirty Dancing*, which eventually also made its way to the stage.

"Part of his world" (chapter 4) reminded me of a song in *The Little Mermaid*, which, similarly started out as a movie and, years later, became a live musical.

"So long ago and so far away" (chapter 6) called to mind a song made popular by **The Carpenters** many years ago, as well as a song from many years earlier, earning an Academy Award nomination for Best Song for its creators, **Jerome Kern** and **Ira Gershwin**. Taken from the film, *Cover Girl*, it was included in at least one musical revue—built around Kern's music—so I think it counts!

"Chemistry . . . yes, chemistry!" (chapter 7) Okay, I cheated on this one for the sake of a little fun. As you probably know, this harkens back to "I'll Know" from *Guys and Dolls*.

"Try as we might" (chapter 7) is a phrase that was used in "Seeing Things" from *The Happy Time*, by **Kander & Ebb.**

"For one night only" (chapter 7) is a common expression used to stir up business for a particular performance or special event, one which was adapted into a song in *Dreamgirls*.

"A cockeyed optimist" (chapter 10) is, of course, a phrase Nellie Forbush uses to describe herself in *South Pacific*.

"Just around the corner somewhere" (chapter 10) actually calls to mind two different songs in *West Side Story*!

"Dear friend" (chapter 11) is actually the title of a song from the lovely musical, *She Loves Me*.

"We decided just to wait . . . and wait . . . and wait . . ." (chapter 13) Another one where I embellished my thought for the purpose of testing your musical acumen. Anyone familiar with *Follies* will recognize this comes from "Waiting Around for the Girls Upstairs.'

"Old friends" (chapter 13) is a song title from another **Sondheim** musical, *Merrily We Roll Along*.

I had to "review the situation" (chapter 19) before meeting **Ethel Merman**. *Oliver!* came to mind!

"Nowadays" (chapter 23), like "tradition," is another single word that, all by itself, can evoke a show, in this case *Chicago*.

"I've always been shy" (chapter 26), even prior to the creation of *Once Upon a Mattress*, which features a song bearing this lyric.

"The most unusual ways" (chapter 26) called to mind a song with a similar title in the musical, *Nine*.

"My practical list of 'don'ts" (chapter 28) is even more practical than Laurey's in "People Will Say We're In Love" in *Oklahoma!*

"Moment to moment" (chapter 29) is a phrase that's sung in a little-known song, "Whoever You Are," from the well-known musical, *Promises, Promises*.

"Miracle of miracles" (chapter 31) describes my encounter with "Mrs. Anna," as well as Motel's delight in his prospects for the future in *Fiddler On the Roof*.

"This is the moment" (chapter 31) is the title of a great song from *Jekyll and Hyde*.

"Small talk" (chapter 31) is a delightful duet from *The Pajama Game*.

"Just in time" (chapter 32) is perhaps the best-known song from *Bells Are Ringing*.

"Life upon the wicked stage" (chapter 32) is my third—and final—purposeful homage to a song, this one coming from the classic, *Show Boat*.

Wouldn't you know it? The very last line in the book proper (chapter 33) turns out to be yet another musical reference, this one calling to mind the opening number—the title song—from *Company*.

BIBLIOGRAPHY

Bloom, Ken. *Show and Tell: The New Book of Broadway Anecdotes.* New York: Oxford, 2016.

Ewen, David. *Complete Book of the American Musical Theater.* New York: Henry Holt and Company, 1959.

Facebook. facebook.com.

Internet Broadway Database. Ibdb.com.

Kantor, Adam. 'My Long Journey From Anatevka to 'Fiddler' On Broadway." Forward, January 26, 2016.

McNeil, Alex. *Total Television.* New York: Penguin, 1991.

Phoenix. Student Press, Inc.

Queens Chronicle. New York: Mark I Publications, Inc.

Reader's Encyclopedia, The. New York: Thomas Y. Crowell Company, 1965.

Sheward, David. *It's a Hit!* New York: Watson-Guptill Publications, 1994.

Stevenson, Isabelle. *The Tony Award*. New York: Crown, 1987.

Wikipedia. wikipedia.org.

Willis, John and Ben Hodges. *Theatre World*. New York: Crown, Applause, Theatre World Media. Multiple volumes.

INDEX

ABOUT THE AUTHOR

Mark Lord was born in Brooklyn and raised in Puerto Rico, where his lifelong devotion to the theater began. He is a retired New York City public school teacher, a freelance journalist and an enthusiastic participant in community theater—as an actor, director and playwright.

Several of his plays have been produced, including *Let's Hear It For Queens*, a musical tribute to the borough he now calls home, an excerpt of which was published in the anthology, *Act One: One Act Vol. 2* in 2018. This is his first published book.